THE LITTLE CORI
FISH AND SEA
COOKBOOK

Beatriz Treloar

WillowOrchard Publishing

A view from the Treloar family farm near Zennor

Introduction

I love seafood. This is probably why I am working in the SEAFOOD ON STILTS restaurant in St Ives. Fish, shellfish, samphire, seaweed all can be found on my menus. We are so lucky living and working here in Cornwall where we have wonderful fresh fish and seafood a stonesthrow from our restaurant door. Growing up on a local farm I am fanatical about fresh seasonal herbs, vegetables and fruit and my family supply us with those daily from just along the coast. So I can always get the freshest ingredients which make the best food.

I know that not everyone has the luxury of the flexibility to be able to spend time buying food, but if you do have butchers, fishmongers, greengrocers or vegetable farms not too far away, I do urge you to try them out if you haven't already, because the difference in flavour from supermarket-bought produce can be amazing. If you like, save the trip for the weekend and get enough to freeze and cook it during the week.

In the restaurant we always include a couple of "non fish" choices on the menu for those who don't eat fish and I have included a few here. Plus some "unfishy" soups and sides and Early Bird options as we all like variety in our lives.

When my partner's younger brother was struggling with health and behavioural issues their mother changed his diet and lo and behold things improved rapidly for him. So with a growing awareness of food intolerances, in this little book I have taken some of my family's favourite meals and substituted ingredients, freeing them from dairy and gluten. Of course, they were originally dairy based so cows' milk, cream, and cheese can replace the goats', sheeps' or plant-based you will find here in equal measures.

My Spanish mother is a brilliant cook and my brother Félipe, and my sisters Eva, Lucia and I were blessed with great food throughout our childhood. The recipes I have chosen for this little book are favourites, many from those early years, others inspired by them, and many appear on the menus in the restaurant.

We were raised as vegetarians and although I now love seafood, and eat meat, game and poultry, you will mostly find seafood and vegetables here.

I hope you will enjoy some of the tastes from the Seafood on Stilts restaurant and my west Cornwall childhood.

Saludos and best wishes.............Beatriz Treloar.

Ingredient notes and measures

For those who do not eat "free from, dairy can be substituted for the goats', sheeps' and plant-based ingredients used here. Plant-based includes oat, soya, coconut, almond and other nuts.

For those with no gluten issues any pastry, bread flours and bread can be used.

For the pasties, Jus Rol make a gluten free pastry variety, but the flaky here is really easy to make.

For the filo in the Eastern rolls, Blue Dragon make gluten free spring roll wrappers

My recipes call for gluten free soy sauce, but feel free to use any soy-sauce if there are no gluten issues.

Where I use groundnut oil, again any flavourless oil such as vegetable, sunflower or rapeseed will work.

A glug = 25 ml

A slug = 40 ml

A splash = 10 ml

...........approximately!

Where I've shown measures in gm and oz and ml and pints, other than in baking where measurements should be more precise, the conversions are not always exact – more for ease of following the recipe from which you will still get a fabulous dish!

MAINS

Two fish pie with prawns

haddock, natural smoked, 1 fillet

ling, 1 fillet (unsmoked haddock or cod will work here too)

shallots, 5, banana, chopped

prawns, cooked, shell off, 1 mugful

parsley, fresh, chopped, 1 large handful

gluten free plain flour, 5 tablespoons

goats' butter, 100g (4oz)

groundnut oil, 1 glug

goats' or plant-based milk, 500ml (1 pint)

potatoes, 4 medium, unpeeled

3 – 4 portions

Start by caramelising the shallots well, which will take 30 – 45 minutes. Heat a small saucepan over a medium heat then add the groundnut oil and turn the heat right down and add the shallots, stirring. Basically all you need to do now is leave them, stirring occasionally, until they are a rich dark brown colour – they will cook in their own juices and become sweet.

With the shallots caramelising, start to boil the potatoes. Now poach the fish in the goats' or plant-based milk; add the goats' or plant-based milk to a medium sized pan or wok, with a lid, and bring to the boil, add the ling and smoked haddock and simmer with the lid on for 3 – 4 minutes, until the skin can be easily removed from the fillets. Remove the fish, pull off the skin and discard, set the liquor aside and break up the fish into chunky pieces.

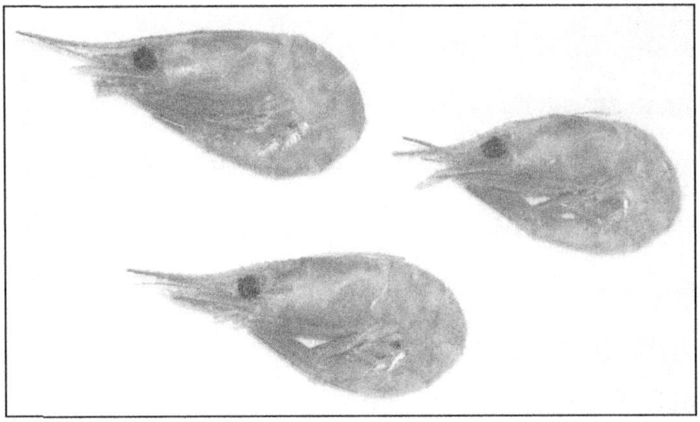

When the potatoes are cooked, make the mash. First rice the potatoes then fork them until fluffy, or if you don't have a ricer, peel them and use a masher or the back of a fork. Then add half the goats' butter and 4 – 5 tablespoons of the fish / goats' or plant-based milkliquor.

Now, melt the remaining goats' butter in a large saucepan over a medium heat then add the gluten free plain flour, stirring constantly for 5 minutes, then add the rest of the fish liquor, stirring well with a wooden spoon until you have a creamy sauce. Simmer to thicken for around 10 minutes, stirring occasionally. Add the fish, shallots, parsley, and prawns, stirring for a further 3 minutes. Pour into a pie dish and allow to cool for 20 – 25 minutes, to allow to set a little, and put the oven on to pre-heat to 180°C fan / gas mark 6.

When the fish mix has solidified a little, spoon the potato on top and gently flatten it, creating swirling patterns with a fork to make the finished dish more attractive, then place on the middle shelf of the oven for 35 – 45 minutes, when the potato will have turned a lovely golden brown.

Remove from the oven and carefully serve the dish using a large kitchen spoon to keep the potato intact over the fantastically tasty creamy fish and prawns.

Anyfish cakes

crabmeat, white, 2 handfuls, around 100g (4oz)

firm fish - monkfish, ling, cod, haddock, or conger eel, around 100g (4oz)

large uncooked prawns, 4, shells removed, black tract removed

medium potato, boiled and riced or crushed, 1

egg yolk, 1

white pepper, 2 – 3 good pinches to taste

fresh parsley, chopped, ½ handful

chilli powder, 1 generous pinch (or 1 teaspoon of fresh chilli chopped)

salt, 2 good pinches

groundnut oil, 1 glug

goats' butter, 1 knob

portions, 2 – 4 depending on how hungry you are

For this dish I prefer monkfish because of its density and texture, but it really can be made with any firm fish – hence its name and the suggestions of other fish as alternatives.

Put the oven on to 160°C fan / gas mark 4

Skin the fish (if the skin is still on) and place it in a medium heated pan with groundnut oil, turning every 30 seconds or so, then add the shelled prawns after around 5 minutes.

Continue turning the fish and prawns for another 5 minutes then remove them from the pan and chop them coarsely before putting them into a bowl.

Put the potato into another bowl and mix in the white pepper a bit at a time until you're satisfied the pepper taste will come through without being too powerful. Don't forget that when you add the potato /pepper mix to the other ingredients the pepperiness will be diluted.

Add the potato / pepper mix to the fish, then add the crabmeat, parsley, and chilli powder, and stir the mixture before adding the egg yolk and mixing well. Now form into round cakes – 65mm (2½") across and around 20mm (¾") thick, firming them as you shape. You can never be quite sure how many cakes you'll end up with but it will probably be 4 – 6.

Heat a pan to moderate heat and add the goats' butter. When fizzing has subsided add the cakes and sizzle away. As the ingredients are already cooked you are cooking now for colour and crispness, which should take just 3 – 4 minutes per side for the cakes to turn a lovely golden brown colour. Don't overcook them as they will become too dry Put the cakes in the oven to heat through thoroughly – about 15 minutes..

These cakes are very good as a starter, or try as a main with braised fennel and roasted tomatoes. They are also fantastic with poached eggs for breakfast.

Aubergine and roquefort sandwich

aubergine, ripe, 1

roquefort 6oz (150g), soft (ripe) or any soft blue goats' or sheeps' cheese

4 portions, try 2 hot, and 2 cold later

Put the oven on to 180°C fan / gas mark 6.

When you've finished slicing the aubergine you're going to reassemble it, so keep it together as you're slicing to make the next part easier. Slice the aubergine lengthways into strips around 7mm (1/4") thick, then spread the ripe roquefort on the top side of each slice, apart from the very top piece, and reassemble. If you've got any goats' or sheeps' cheese left over, just eat it – chef's treat! I always seem to end up with a slice around 12mm (1/2") wide, lovely on its own.

Then simply place on a piece of foil which should be folded into a secure parcel, put on a baking tray and put in a hot oven for 45 minutes. Easy-peasy. Also delicious sliced cold as a starter or snack.

Move onto chopping board and slice from top to bottom with a serrated knife and serve (1 sandwich gives 8 slices). Juices from foil should be poured over sandwich when plated up. If you're leaving any to try cold, leave in one piece in fridge and slice when ready.

Beautifully creamy and laced with blue highlights inside.

This is also a great dish for the barbeque. – put parcel on grill over very hot coals, and still cook it for 45 minutes, but turn it after 20. Make the parcel leak proof otherwise the juices will leak out when you turn at half time. If they do, quickly and carefully wrap in more foil.

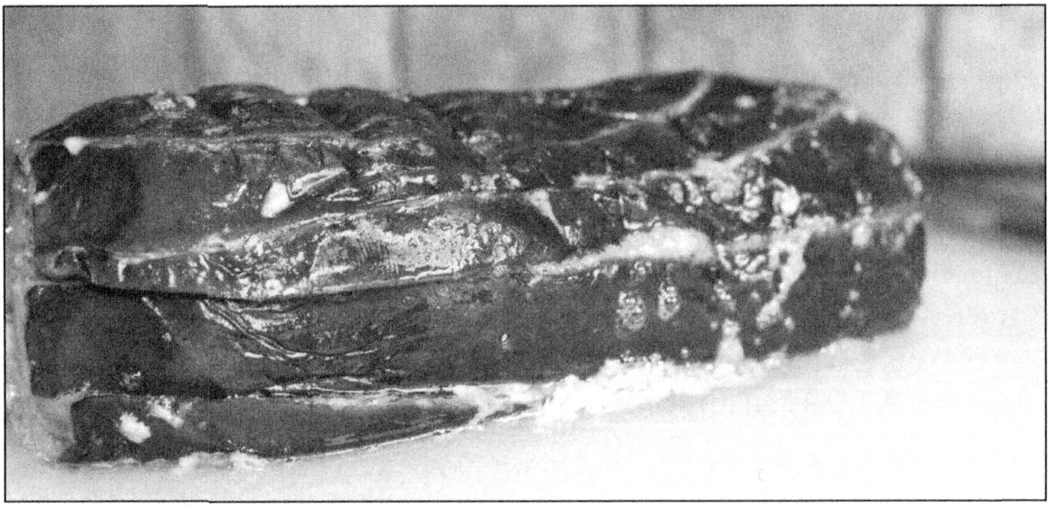

An intriguing dark toasted purple outside.

Cod, baked in parcels with basil and lemon

cod fillet, 1 large or 2 small, skinned and cut into bite-sized pieces

lemon, 1, thinly sliced

basil leaves, 12

salt, 2 pinches

2 portions

This is an easy to prepare and quick to cook dish. Goes well with mashed potatoes (try roasted tomato mash) and steamed broccoli.

Preheat the oven to 170°C fan / gas mark 5. Simply take the cod and make a layer, around 100mm – 125mm (4" – 5") square on a good-sized piece of kitchen foil and sprinkle salt over. Place a layer of lemon on top, then a few of the basil leaves and repeat until all the ingredients are used up.

Then just bring the edges of the foil together, fold over and crimp together to keep the steam in, and place in the oven on a baking tray for 30 minutes. Take out, unfold the foil carefully (don't scald yourself on the steam inside), and serve.

Conger eel and prawns – Eastern style

conger eel (or any firm white fish such as monkfish) steaks, 3, skin and bone removed, cut into bite sized pieces

king prawns, 12, raw, shells removed

lime leaves, 2, finely chopped with woody centre stems removed

chilli, orange, 1 (use red if you can't get orange), finely chopped, no seeds

garlic, 1 clove, peeled and crushed

ginger, 1 generous thumb, peeled and grated

sheeps' or goats' yoghurt, 2 tablespoons

spring onions, 6, topped and tailed, sliced

beansprouts, 2 handfuls, soaked in salted water for 1 hour then dried

tomatoes, 4, medium, chopped with woody bits removed

toasted sesame oil, 2 glugs

salt, to taste

2 portions

I always think the mix of fish with tomatoes is a really good combination, and this dish is no exception. Lots of people don't like dishes too spicy hot, especially seafood, but if you do like it hot, then leave the seeds with the chilli as you chop. Also, if you want a stronger flavour of toasted sesame put in more toasted sesame oil.

Gently stir fry the chilli, lime leaves, garlic, and ginger in the oil for 5 minutes over a medium heat, to infuse the oil with their flavours. Turn up the heat to medium and when the oil is hot add the conger, prawns and tomatoes and stir-fry gently for 5 minutes, then add the beansprouts and spring onions. Stir-fry for 3 minutes then add the sheeps' or goats' yoghurt; stir gently for 3 more minutes to heat through again and serve.

The dish is great on its own but also goes very well with egg noodles or rice if you want something a bit more filling.

Courgettes, fried in goats' butter with mustard seeds

courgettes, 2, topped and tailed, chunkily sliced

goats' butter, 1 good knob, around 50g (2oz)

mustard seeds, 2 teaspoons

2 portions

This is an easy, and quick but different, way of cooking courgettes. It is not particularly spicy, which makes it suitable for any dish where you would normally think about using a steamed vegetable (or even boiled).

Put a medium sized pan over a medium heat and when hot, add the goats' butter. When the goats' butter has melted add the mustard seeds and stir, then add the courgettes. Leave them for around 6 - 8 minutes, stirring and tasting for crunchiness occasionally, then serve.

Told you this was another easy one.

Crab fishcakes; zingy plain or with tomato or smoked haddock.

Basic

crabmeat, mixed brown and white meat, around 150g or 6oz

cod, or smoked haddock small, ½ fillet, skin removed, finely chopped (depending on version)

chilli, red, small, 1, seeds removed, finely chopped (or 2, depending on option)

ginger, 1 thumb, peeled and grated

lemon zest, grated, 2 teaspoons

coriander leaves, 1 handful, chopped (or 3 depending on option)

garlic, 1 clove, finely chopped

goats' butter, 1 knob

eggs, 2, beaten

breadcrumbs, fresh, 2 handfuls (you can finely chop a thick slice of my gluten free soda bread, see page 126)

salt to taste

strawberries, 2 small portions (4 to 6 for each depending on size), sliced

or eggs, 4, for frying or poaching

groundnut oil. 2 glugs

balsamic vinegar, 1 good glug

tomatoes, cherry, 4, for smoked haddock version

2 portions

For the crab fishcakes. if you like a hot and more Eastern tasting cake, try the tomato, chilli and coriander, or for a smoky version, use natural smoked haddock rather than the cod.

With tomato chilli and coriander - Add 4 cherry tomatoes, chopped, 1 extra chilli, fine chopped, and 2 extra handfuls of chopped coriander leaves at the first frying stage.

With smoked haddock - Use ½ fillet of natural smoked haddock instead of cod

2 portions

Preheat the oven to 160°C fan / gas mark 4.

Place a medium saucepan over medium heat, and when hot add 1 glug of oil and when that is hot add crabmeat, cod, chilli and coriander, then fry, stirring, for 5 minutes. Add lemon zest, ginger, chilli and garlic, mix well, fry for one more minute. Remove from the pan, set aside in a bowl to cool. When cool add the beaten eggs and breadcrumbs to the mixture, and mix well before forming into 8 cakes, flattened and a bit less than 2cm, or ¾ inch, thick. Put the cakes on a plate, cling, place in the fridge for 30 minutes to let the cakes harden; it makes them easier to get into the pan for cooking and also keep their shape.

Heat the second glug of oil in a frying pan, when hot add the goats' butter, and when melted, add the cakes and just smell the fantastic aromas. Fry for 3 minutes then turn. The upper side should be golden brown; if not, cook 2nd side for 4 minutes and turn to fry again for 1 minute at the end. Place in the oven to heat through for 10 minutes.

While finishing the cakes in the oven prepare the serving dishes by placing sliced strawberries on them and drizzling the balsamic vinegar over. When cooked, neatly place the cakes by their side – looks and tastes fantastic.

With eggs, fried or poached

If there are one or two cakes left over from supper, try them with fried or poached eggs for breakfast.

Eastern seafood rolls

I have included this recipe because it is my partner Jory's absolute favourite and very popular in the restaurant. Yes, I know, most filo pastry contains gluten, but you could always use my gluten free pastry, see page 124, to make little pasties. Blue Dragon make gluten free spring roll wrappers.

There are 3 sets of ingredients:

For the fishy part

Monkfish, properly skinned with membrane removed, cut into 15 small cubes (6mm, ¼")

king prawns, 15, shell off, black tract removed, uncooked

white crabmeat, 1 handful (75g – 100g, 3oz – 4oz)

ginger, half a thumb, peeled and cut into very fine matchsticks

toasted sesame oil, 2 good glugs

For the flavouring part

red chilli, small, 1, seeds in, finely chopped

lime, 1, grated zest of

shallot, large, 1, finely chopped

garlic, 1 clove, peeled and crushed

toasted sesame oil, 1 glug

For the finishing part

coriander leaves fresh, 1 good handful

creamed coconut, 1 tablespoon, grated if necessary

filo pastry – half a sheet per seafood roll, cut in half lengthways (remove from packet and cut at the last minute, or it will dry out) or side plate sized rounds of gluten free pastry

sweet chilli dipping sauce, 2 small pots

toasted sesame oil, 1 good glug

groundnut oil, 1 good glug

2 portions (6 rolls)

Fishy part

Heat 1 glug of the oil. When hot fry monkfish until golden brown (around 5 minutes), set aside on kitchen towel to dry. Wipe pan, heat last glug of oil until hot, fry king prawns until pink (2 – 3 minutes), remove, drain and dry on kitchen towel. When cool cut prawns into small pieces. Put prawns and monkfish with other fishy part ingredients into bowl, mix well.

The flavouring part

Gently fry all ingredients in oil until soft or lightly browned, drain and dry on kitchen towel.

Finishing the rolls

Preheat the oven to 170°C fan / gas mark 5

Add the flavouring part to the fishy part and mix well, then add the coriander and creamed coconut and mix in thoroughly. Make up first roll by putting one sixth of the mixture at the end and in the centre of the first piece of filo, fold the sides in so they overlap the mixture, then roll up from the end that the mixture is at. Repeat for the other 5 rolls. If using the gluten free pastry just form as little pasties.

Add the sesame and groundnut oils to a frying pan, heat until hot, add the rolls, turn frequently, cooking until golden brown (4 – 5 minutes). Keep an eye on them, because when they begin to colour, they go quickly. Dry, on kitchen towel. For the gluten free pasty version, place in the heated oven for 30 minutes. Serve, with small bowls of dipping sauce on the side.

Fishy filo parcels with pak choi

cod medium, ½ fillet, thick end, skin removed, cut into bite sized pieces

haddock medium, ½ fillet, thick end, skin removed, cut into bite sized pieces

prawns, shells removed, uncooked, 1 handful

pak choi, 2, leaves separated, longer ones cut in half lengthways

spring onions, 4, sliced, fried in sesame oil, dried

potatoes, peeled, 1 large or 4 small, par boiled, diced into 6mm (¼") cubes

filo pastry, 1 sheet per parcel; don't removed from packaging until using or they'll dry out

light yeast and preservative free soy sauce for drizzling over cod and haddock to marinate

2 portions, 4 parcels

This is very popular in the restaurant so I include it here even though it isn't gluten free.

One of the pleasures of this dish is building the parcels from the assembled ingredients, so the key is to get them all ready for the composition!

The potatoes will take from 10 – 15 minutes to par-boil depending on how small the potatoes or chunks are. You don't want them too soft or they'll lose their texture when they're cooking on in the parcel. When they're ready, dry them then chop into small dice and set aside.

Remove the skin from the cod and haddock, cut the fillets into two, and keep the thick end of each. Put the thinner ends in the freezer, ready to use for a fishcakes or stock later. To get the most out of these parcels you really need the thicker end to maintain a good texture. Cut the ½ fillets into bite size chunks and drizzle with the yeast and preservative free soy, 15 minutes before assembling the parcels. Turn on oven to preheat to 170°C fan / gas mark 5.

On a floured surface lay out two sheets of pastry, cut into 4 equal squares, and put a few leaves of pak choi, a quarter of the total for each parcel, in the centre of each, next to one another – making squares of them around 10cm x 10cm (4" by 4"), with two layers, the top criss-crossing the bottom.

Then add a fishy layer, mixing the cod, haddock, and prawns, laying the chunks over the leaves, then a layer of potatoes, and then a layer of spring onions. Repeat until all the ingredients are used up with a final layer of pak choi on top if you have enough.

Holding carefully to avoid ripping, fold in the sides of each piece of filo to the centre and crimp together to finish make into parcels. It doesn't matter if they don't look pretty or symmetrical, when they're cooked they'll look fabulous.

Have the oven ready, preheated to 170°C fan / gas mark 5, put the parcels onto an oiled baking tray, then brush them with beaten egg to give them a lovely golden hue when cooked, and put into the oven.

Leave in the oven for around 10 - 15 minutes and take out when the pastry looks great. Keep an eye out though, you don't want the pastry burning or the fish to lose that chunky texture.

Serve hot, BUT THESE FISHY PARCELS AREN'T HALF BAD COLD EITHER.

Fish pasty

cod, haddock, or monkfish, uncooked, skinned, 300g - 400g (¾lb – 1lb), bite-sized pieces; other chunky white fish works; mixed fish too if that's what you have (**NO** oily fish).

celery, 2 sticks, stringy fibres pulled or peeled, chopped, sliced

shallots, 2, or onion, medium, 1, rough chopped

potato, large, 1, peeled, diced

mushy peas, 6 – 8 tablespoons, for ingredients and method see below

gluten free flaky pastry, 480gm, just over 1lb, split to two portions and rolled into 2 x 250mm (10") circles.

for my pastry method and ingredients to make your own go to *Gluten Free Baking* and page 124.

salt, 2 teaspoons

white pepper, lots, to taste

egg, 1 beaten

for the mushy peas method go to my mushy recipe on page 81 in *Sauces and Sides*. Here's what you'll need:

marrowfat peas, dried (NOT quick soak type,) 1 packet, soaked for 12 hours, allow another ¾ - 1 hour to cook (well worth the effort!)

onion, 1, peeled and chopped

garlic cloves, 2, whole, peeled

thyme stalks, 4 – 5 around 100mm (4") long

goats' butter, around 50g (2oz)

water, 1½ - 2 litres (3 – 4 pints)

2 portions, 2 pasties

First preheat oven to 170°C / gas mark 5 while you're preparing the pasties.

Lay the fish pieces on a sheet of kitchen towel, place another sheet on top and gently press down and rotate to dry them off. Prepare pastry by pressing into two balls on a gluten free plain floured board or work-top, then flatten a little with palm of your hand and roll (with gluten free plain floured rolling pin) until you have 2 circles approximately 250 mm (10") in diameter.

Mix celery and shallot or onion together and lay half the mixture in a line 50mm – 75mm (2" – 3") wide across the middle of each circle of pastry (from left to right as you look at them), running up to around 50mm (1") of each edge and increasing in height in the middle. Lay the fish pieces on top of the celery shallot mix, and if you're using different fish, keep them separate as you lay the pieces, so you can see if you can taste the difference as you bite through. Now, give a good sprinkling of white pepper, then sprinkle salt over.

Layer potato pieces over the fish in each pasty and spoon 3 – 4 tablespoons of mushy peas over the potato pieces. Give another good sprinkling of white pepper.

Brush egg around the edges of the pastry, so the pasties hold together when cooking. Now form the first pasty. Lift the edges furthest away and nearest to you and crimp them by bringing the edges together, holding them with your forefingers and thumbs. Then, using your thumbs, roll the edge nearest over the top of the edge furthest away and then roll it a little further so the edge furthest away has been tucked under and behind the edge originally nearest to you. Now move your fingers and thumbs to the left and repeat, then again and again until you've reached the end of the pasty. Then go back to the middle and repeat the exercise moving to the right this time until you have a complete pasty.

Don't worry too much if there are gaps in your crimping or splits in the pastry – it would be amazing if there weren't. If the gaps are small just press the pastry together to close them. For larger gaps brush the edges with egg and cover them with small pieces of rolled pastry, pressing the edges together or rubbing the two surfaces into one another as best you can. Brush the pasties with beaten egg.

For those of us who don't do this every day, crimping pasties is a far from perfect science; sometimes you'll be left with a perfect closure, and sometimes your pasties will need a bit of patching up. As long as the pasties are more or less completely closed you'll have done your job and the ingredients will reach that perfect melange that you're looking for.

Brush the pasties with the egg, place on an oiled baking tray and put on the middle shelf until the pasties are a delicious golden brown, which will take 40 – 45 minutes.

Remove from the oven and serve straight away. These are fabulous on their own .... THE THING THAT MAKES THESE FISH PASTIES IS THE MUSHY PEAS. A VARIATION ON A TRADITIONAL FISH AND CHIP SUPPER.

Fish ball feast

cod fillet, small, skinned, keep skin

red mullet, filleted, skinned, keep skin and frame (head, tail, and bones)

prawns, shell on, large, uncooked, shelled, 6, retain heads and shells

red gurnard, filleted, skinned, keep skin and frame (head, tail and bones)

monkfish steak, ½, keep bone

coriander, fresh, 1 handful, include stalks

tomatoes, small, 12

new potatoes, small, 8 – 10, skin on, whole

shallots, 10, peeled, whole

good basil sprigs, 4

vanilla pod, 1

bay leaves, with stem on, 4

onion, 1, peeled and medium chopped

egg yolk, 1, beaten

breadcrumbs, fresh, 2 tablespoons. 1 slice of soda bread fine chopped should do it. Why not make your own using my recipe on page 127 in *Gluten Free Baking*

gluten free plain flour, 6 tablespoons on board or flat dish

4 portions

First blanch the tomatoes, remove skins and chop, removing the woody bits. Then, make a stock using 2 pints of water; add the fish frames, and skins, prawn heads and shells, and the tomatoes and onion. Bring to the boil then simmer for 45 minutes before taking from the heat and sieving the liquor over a soup pan. Set the liquor aside, discard the rest.

While the stock is simmering make up a bouquet garni by tying the vanilla pod, bay leaves and basil stems together.

Mix breadcrumbs and egg yolk in bowl, chop fish and prawns finely, add to bowl and mix. Scoop out in 3 – 4 tablespoon portions and roll into small balls, set aside as they are completed.

Now put the stock over a medium heat and bring to a simmer, then add the bouquet garni, potatoes and shallots. Simmer for 10 minutes. Gently roll fish balls in the gluten free plain flour to give light coating before laying them gently on top of the sauce.

Simmer gently for 20 minutes with lid on, and your poached fishballs are ready to go. Don't worry if the balls have broken up, the flavour will still be delicious.

A flowering sprig of Choi Sum adds a bright touch to the dish

Monkfish and tomato curry

monkfish fillet, around 400g (1lb), cubed into around 18 bite-sized pieces

large prawns, raw, peeled, 6, black tracts removed, each chopped into 3 pieces

crabmeat, white, 1 good handful (around 150g, or 6oz)

fresh tomatoes, small, ripe, 10

coconut cream, 1 tin, 400ml (¾ pint)

okra, 12

coriander, fresh, 2 handfuls, chopped

potato, medium, 1 peeled and small diced

curry masala, 1 desert spoon

red chilli, ½ - 1, chopped, seeds in or out to taste

ginger, 2 thumbs, peeled and grated

garlic, crushed, 2 cloves

lime or lemon leaves, 2 medium, stalks removed, fine chopped

onion, 1, peeled and medium chopped

salt, 4 good pinches

toasted sesame oil, 2 good glugs

2 portions

The key thing with this dish is to make sure the sauce is creamy, with the tomatoes part of the creaminess, and well reduced. Cooking time for the sauce alone is at least an hour to an hour and a half (the longer the better – if you can cook it for two hours, then great). Bearing in mind the preparation time, this dish can take three hours to deliver to the table.

The tomatoes should have their skins on and be chopped, with the woody bit in the middle at the top removed. Make sure you don't lose any juice, so prepare them on a board with a runnel around the edge.

With chillies, because you can usually not tell in advance how hot they are going to be, start by adding half the amount, then testing for heat after a while to see if you need to add more – you can always add heat but it is hard to remove it.

Heat a wok to medium heat then add the oil; when hot add the onion, garlic, ginger, lime leaves, chilli, and curry masala and fry for 5 – 6 minutes, stirring frequently.

Now add ¾ of the coconut milk and crabmeat and simmer for 15 minutes, still stirring frequently, then the tomatoes. Continue stirring every few minutes. If you don't, there is a danger the mixture at the bottom of the pan will stick and burn.

When the mixture begins to resemble a sauce (after 30 - 45 minutes) add the remaining oil and coconut milk, and the salt.

After another 10 minutes add the potato and simmer the mixture until the potato is medium soft, which will probably take around 15 - 20 minutes, then add the monkfish. Simmer for a further 15 minutes when the monkfish will be almost cooked then add the prawns, coriander and okra. Just leave for 5 – 6 minutes, still stirring, then serve. Don't be afraid to add a bit of water if you think it's getting too dry at any stage, or cook for a little longer for the potatoes to soften a little more – different varieties can take different amounts of time to cook.

A fabulous dish, rich and filling, this is great on its own. So many flavours come through.

Mushy pea and cheese bites

This recipe was devised for the Treloar family's annual May Day party by our great friend Dr Anthony Tremayne and is now an essential at any bash.

mushy peas, 2 tablespoons per bite (ingredients and recipe notes below)

hard goats' or sheeps' cheese, small diced, 2 tablespoon per bite

onion, chopped, 1 tablespoon per bite

flaky pastry, 480 gm, just over 1lb. To make your own follow my recipe on page 124 in *Gluten Free Baking*

egg, 1, beaten

For the peas (follow the method on page 81 in *Sauces and Sides):*

marrowfat peas, dried, 1 packet (250g or 10oz), soaked for 12 hours and rinsed in cold water, (NOT quick soak type – doctor's orders!)

onion, 1, peeled and fine chopped

garlic cloves, 2, peeled, whole

thyme, fresh, 4 – 5 stalks, whole, around 10cm (4") long

goats' butter, around 50g (2oz)

water, 1½ - 2 litres (3 – 4 pints)

salt to taste

white pepper to taste

water, to cover peas as they cook

portion control is up to you – as many as you have pastry and ingredients for!

Preheat the oven to 180°C / gas mark 6

Liberally flour your rolling surface, rolling pin, and dough, and keep sprinkling the dough with flour as you roll to avoid sticking and roll out the pastry thinly. Cut 15cm (around 5") diameter circles using a saucer as a guide, then place the ingredients in the centre of each. Spoon the peas on the bottom, then layer the goats' or sheeps' cheese and finally spoon the onions on top of the cheese.

Lift the edges furthest away from and nearest to you together, then squeeze them together with your fingers, and roll them over so that the edges are sealed. (As gluten free pastry can be quite fragile carefully use a pallet knife to free the circles from the surface if they are sticking).

Finish off with a brushing of beaten egg and put into a medium oven for around 30 minutes. They may take a little shorter or longer depending on the final size of your bites and the thickness of the pastry. Just cook until the pastry is golden brown.

Allow to cool for a few minutes as the filling will be extremely hot, then devour. These are best eaten warm, so if there are any left over, it is best to re-heat them (wrapped in foil in a hot oven for 15 minutes) rather than eating them cold.

Mussels poached in cider with chorizo thyme and leek

Yes, chorizo is meat but just leave it out if you don't eat meat. I put this recipe in for my dearest friend Ochre Pengelly, who loves this dish and drew the little sketches in this book in exchange for a very large portion.

mussels, 2 litres (4 pints)

chorizo, uncooked, 1 fat finger, small diced (3mm, 1/8") (optional)

dry Cornish cider, apple , 500ml (1 pint)

thyme stalks, fresh, 2 good handfuls (LOTS - looks like too much!)

leek, medium, ½, small chopped

garlic, 1 clove, peeled

goats' butter, 1 knob

bread of choice

2 large portions

I know this sounds like a very unlikely list of ingredients, but it really does work so incredibly and surprisingly well that you won't be able to wait to do it the next time! If you have hand-picked the mussels yourself (if there is an R in the month), they'll taste even better.

First heat a pan over a low heat, and without oil add the chorizo. Sweat it in its own fat for around 5 – 6 minutes. Keep an eye on it - too long and it will burn, becoming bitter. Strain from pan, leave on kitchen towel to drain. DO NOT use fat from chorizo with the mussels; it will discolour them, and your fingers when you eat them!

Heat a big saucepan that has a lid - and that doesn't have a coating that needs care - over a medium heat and when hot add the goats' butter, then the leeks and stir fry for 1 minute; then add the chorizo and garlic, stir fry for 3 minutes. Add the cider and turn the heat up to high.

When bubbling, add the mussels, discarding any that won't close stir them about to coat all in the poaching liquor, put the lid on the pan. After

2 minutes stir them about again, very well and replace the lid. They will be cooked after another 2 minutes.

Serve, spooning chorizo pieces, leek, and thyme sprigs into bowls and use the bread to dip into the delicious liquor. Discard any mussels that haven't opened.

The first time, you'll be very pleasantly surprised you cooked your mussels this way; the second time, you'll probably be surprised that you had remembered your thoughts correctly from the first time!

From low tide mark on the beach

To cleaned and waiting for the pan

Natural smoked haddock with milk sauce and poached egg

natural smoked haddock fillet, 1 large, or 2 small, skin removed, cut into 2 portions

goats' or plant-based milk, whole, 1 pint

onion, small, ½, finely chopped

goats' butter, very generous knob (around 50gm /2 oz should be fine)

saffron, 1 very good pinch

gluten free plain flour, 1 teaspoon

white wine vinegar, 1 dash

2 eggs

2 portions

Slowly melt goats' butter in a large pan and then add onion, frying gently until soft and translucent (around 5 minutes). Add goats' or plant-based milk and saffron; bring to slow simmer then add the haddock, cut into two portions.

Cover pan and gently poach fish for 4 minutes. Gently remove fish, drain it into pan, place in cold water to stop it cooking, and set aside to warm through again later.

Put gluten free plain flour in mug, add 2 teaspoons of water, stir until you have made a thick paste.

Continue to simmer liquor until reduced to around one third of original volume and the saffron has given it a beautiful golden yellow tint, then add gluten free plain flour paste and stir continuously to stop it going lumpy, until the sauce has thickened.

Bring a pan of water to the boil, and add the vinegar. Remove from the heat, stir with a large spoon and while the water is still swirling crack open the eggs and add them gently to the water. Put back onto the heat and poach until cooked, which will take from 2 to 3 minutes depending on how fresh they are.

Add the haddock to another pan of slowly simmering water and warm through, taking another 1 – 2 minutes, which will also finish the cooking.

Now, gently lift the fish from the water, dry using kitchen towel and put on plates. Gently remove the eggs, dry them using kitchen towels, and place them on top of the haddock pieces. Then simply spoon the delicious fish flavoured saffron milk sauce over the eggs and take to the table.

Potatoes baked in stock with spring onions and garlic

potatoes, 2, peeled and thinly sliced

spring onions, 4 topped and tailed, diagonally sliced into 12mm (½") pieces

garlic, 1 clove, peeled and finely chopped

vegetable stock, ½ litre (1 pint)

good olive oil, 2 glugs

salt, to taste

2 portions

This is a very flexible dish, going with many fish dishes.

Start by preheating the oven to 180°C / gas mark 6, then build the dish. Take a medium sized baking dish, around 20cm in diameter by 5cm high (8" x 2"), and put a layer of potatoes at the bottom and sprinkle with salt. Sprinkle some of the garlic evenly over the potatoes, then place a layer of spring onions. Repeat until all the ingredients are used, with the top layer being spring onions. Pour the stock gently into the dish, until just covering the top layer of potatoes and washing half way up the sides of the spring onions, then drizzle the olive oil over the onions and potatoes.

Put the dish onto a baking tray and place in the oven for around 45 minutes.

With good watching, the stock will have reduced to just below the level of the top layer of potatoes, giving you a dish with some potatoes that are golden and crispy, and some which are still soft - a good combination of contrasting textures.

Ray wings in milk sauce with coriander and chive mash and mustard fried courgettes

ray / skate wings, fresh, 2

goats' or plant-based milk, whole, 1 pint

small onion, ½ finely chopped

goats' butter, 1 very generous knob (50g, 2oz)

saffron, very good pinch

gluten free plain flour, 1 teaspoon

courgettes, small, 3, sliced

goats' butter, very generous knob (50g, 2 oz)

goats' butter, smaller knob (25g, 1 oz)

mustard seeds, black, 1 tablespoon. Use brown if you don't have black

For the potatoes

potatoes, large, 2

goats' butter, another very generous knob (50g, 2 oz)

goats' or plant-based cream or goats' or plant-based milk, to taste, 4 - 6 tablespoons

salt and white pepper to taste

chives, chopped, 1 handful

coriander, chopped, 1 handful

2 portions

Slowly melt 1 generous knob of goats' butter in a large pan and then add onion, frying gently until soft and translucent (around 5 minutes). Add goats' or plant-based milk and saffron; bring to slow simmer then add the ray or skate wings.

Cover the pan and gently poach wings for 3 minutes. Gently remove the fish, drain it into the pan, place it in cold water to stop it cooking, and set it aside to heat through again later.

Put the gluten free plain flour in mug, add 2 teaspoons of water, stir until you have made a thick paste.

Continue to simmer the milk liquor until reduced to around one third of original volume and the saffron has given it a beautiful golden yellow tint, then add the gluten free flour paste and stir continuously to stop it going lumpy, until the sauce has thickened.

Make the mashed potato, using my recipe on page 79 in *Sauces and Sides* to see how, and add a handful of chopped chives, then another of chopped coriander, stalks and all, but if you just want chopped leaves that's OK, and stir. Warm in the microwave just before serving.

The mustard seeds take around 5 minutes to pop and the courgettes around 5 minutes to cook, so begin cooking them around 10 minutes before you intend to serve. Melt the small knob of goats' butter in a small saucepan, then add the mustard seeds and put on lid. When the popping has finished (around 5 minutes from time of adding them) add the courgettes, leave the lid off. Stir frequently until the courgettes are cooked to your liking; between 3 and 5 minutes depending on whether you like them crunchy or soft.

Add the ray wings to a larger pan of slowly simmering water and heat through for another minute or so, which will also finish the cooking.

Now, gently lift the fish from the water, dry with kitchen towel, put on plates, then add the potato and courgettes and simply spoon the delicious fish flavoured saffron milk sauce over the wings and take to the table.

Red gurnard poached in sublime tomato sauce

tomatoes, very ripe, 15 small or 10 medium

very good olive oil – 10 good glugs

onions, 2 small or 1 medium, peeled, fine chopped

garlic, 4 large or 6 medium cloves, peeled, crushed

red gurnard fillets, around 300g – 400g (12oz – 16oz), skin removed, each sliced into 4 pieces

salt, 3 or 4 good pinches, to taste

black pepper, ground, to taste

portions, 2 – trying this with tarragon mash (mashed potato with finely chopped fresh tarragon) is highly recommended.

Because the sauce can take a couple of hours, and this is made first, allow yourself enough time. The trick is to allow the oil and tomato juices to reduce, until you have a lovely thick consistency – you're looking for it to have the consistency of double cream. If it's nearer to a thick yoghurt don't worry.

This works well with monkfish too; just prep it well and cut it into bite sized pieces.

First slice the tomatoes, fairly thick – around 1 cm (½") - cutting out the woody bits, then chop them into cubes. Ideally use a board with a runnel round the edge so the tomato juice doesn't escape.

Leave the skins on and seeds in – they add to the colour and flavour of the sauce and really aren't a problem in the final dish as they are so tender; you probably won't even notice they are there.

Heat a wok, or large saucepan or deep frying pan if you don't have one, over a medium heat, and when hot add 2 good glugs of the oil. When the oil is hot add the onion and garlic and stir-fry until fairly soft and translucent.

Now add the chopped tomatoes and another four glugs of oil, stir well and gently bring to the boil. Simmer the mixture for up to two hours, stirring every 5 – 10 minutes to avoid sticking.

Also, you'll need to add more oil, a good glug at a time, at intervals to thin the mixture because it really does take a while to develop the right consistency and you don't want it over-reduced. You might get through 100 – 150 ml before the right consistency is developed. Add salt to taste and enough freshly ground black pepper for the flavour to come through. This sauce gets a lot of the flavour from the oil, so don't be afraid to use the quantity suggested here.

Now....you need your best guesswork to work out when the sauce is around 10 minutes from finishing, when you should add the red gurnard. Don't worry too much if it goes in a bit early or late because the fish is quite dense and won't be effected by being a little overcooked; the sauce won't be spoiled by cooking a little longer than necessary either.

So, you'll probably be adding the gurnard around two hours after putting the onions and garlic into the wok.

I know.......**IT SOUNDS EXTRAVAGANT ON THE OIL FRONT, AND TIME.......**but this sauce really is sublime and well worth the time and effort. The tarragon mash goes well.

Seafood stew, Eastern style

fish stock, 750ml (1½ pints), for method see stocks recipe on page 58 in *Soups and Salads*

tomatoes, 8, large, blanched, skinned and woody bits removed, chopped, (+ squeeze skins over a bowl to collect their juice)

onion, medium, 1, peeled and chopped

chilli, red, chopped, seeds in

garlic, 2 cloves, peeled and crushed

creamed coconut, 200g packet, grated

potatoes, medium, 2, peeled, diced into 12mm (½") pieces

scallops, 10

cod, medium fillet, 1, skinned, cut into large chunks

haddock, medium fillet, 1, skinned, cut into large chunks

monkfish, small steak, cut into bite-sized pieces

toasted sesame oil, 4 glugs

coriander leaves, fresh, including stalks, chopped, 2 handfuls

spring onions, 6, topped and tailed, finely sliced

4 portions

For a dish with so many ingredients this is actually fairly quick to prepare, and very easy to cook.

As with the monkfish and tomato curry the key thing with this dish is to make sure the sauce is creamy, with the tomatoes dissolved into the mixture, which becomes well reduced. Also as with the monkfish and tomato curry, cooking time for the sauce can often be from 1 – 2 hours, and bearing in mind the preparation time, this dish can take two and a half hours to deliver to the table

Begin by reducing the stock to about 250ml (½ pint) and set aside – this should take around 30 – 45 minutes. Then heat a wok over a medium heat and when hot, add the oil. When the oil is hot add the onions, half the chilli, and garlic, and fry until the onion is soft and translucent (around 5 minutes). Add the creamed coconut, tomatoes and juice, and reduced stock, bring to the boil, reduce the heat then simmer, stirring every 15 minutes for around an hour to an hour and a half depending on how the reduction is going.

The time taken to reduce to the sauce consistency you're looking for will vary depending on the cooking heat and the amount of liquid used to start with, including the juiciness of the tomatoes, so just keep cooking, adding water if necessary, until you have a proper sauce. As you're cooking, test for heat and add more chilli if necessary. Don't forget though, the sauce will get hotter as it reduces as you're concentrating not only the flavours but also the heat.

When you think you're about 30 minutes away from having a sauce (as opposed to ingredients sitting in tomato juice) add the potatoes and simmer for another 10 minutes, then add the monkfish and simmer for 5 minutes, stirring occasionally. Now add the cod and haddock and simmer for 5 more minutes then add the scallops and chopped coriander and simmer for 5 more minutes when this feast of flavours will be finished.

Stir gently once the fish has been added to reduce the chances of it breaking up.

Serve in bowls and garnish with the spring onions.

Variegated chillies, grown at home, in the purple stage!

For Eastern style spiciness, dried lime leaves, or even lemon leaves if you can get them, add a touch of authenticity, alongside the ginger, chilli and fresh coriander. Add them with the ginger. I don't always use garlic, well OK about 2% of the time I don't! Seriously though, sometimes garlic can overpower other flavours so in those cases cooks need to be aware that it needs to be used sparingly.

Sublime tomato sauce

This is a wonderful, flexible sauce, great with pasts for those guests who don't eat fish.

tomatoes, ripe, medium, 16, skin on, chopped with woody bits removed

garlic, 4 – 6 cloves depending on size, peeled and crushed

good olive oil, 8 - 10 glugs

onion, 1, medium, fine chopped

salt, to taste

black pepper, fresh ground, lots

portions – depends on how you're using this amazing sauce. Around 4.

This is basically a reduction of the liquid in the tomatoes and the oil, and it will take around two hours to make, on a low to medium light. It needs to simmer softly rather than boil.

Tip: When preparing this quantity of tomatoes, do it on one of those chopping boards with a channel round the edge and a collecting sump, to avoid getting juice all over your work surface – and having less to cook with!

Heat a wok or large saucepan over a medium heat, then add 2 - 3 glugs of the oil; it provides a lot of the flavour to this sauce, so don't be mean with it.

When the oil is warmed, add the onions and garlic and cook slowly until soft and translucent (after around 5 minutes) when you should add the tomatoes.

Every 15 minutes or so give it a stir and add a bit more oil, until it is all used up. The sauce is ready when you have the consistency of double cream. The skins will have coloured the sauce beautifully, and the taste will be amazing. Now just add salt to taste and enough fresh ground black pepper for the flavour to come through.

This is a perfect accompaniment to a wide range of fish, which can even be poached in the sauce as it nears the end of its cooking time and it is great with pasta.

You can make an Eastern version of this fantastic sauce by adding a couple of glugs of toasted sesame oil in place of some of the olive oil, adding chopped fresh chilli to taste, and a couple of lime leaves, chopped, with the central stalk removed.

Chunky tomatoes to begin with

Nicely melded after a couple of hours

Spicy seafood chowder

huss fillet, 1 (or 2) steak, skin removed (but retained) and chopped into bite size pieces

cod fillet, 1, skin removed (but retained) and chopped into bite size pieces

ling fillet, 1, skin removed (but retained) and chopped into bite size pieces

scallops, 6 cut in half

king prawns, bought uncooked shell-on, 9, heads, shells and black vein removed (retain heads and shells), cut in three pieces

onion, medium, 1 peeled and chopped

garlic, 2 cloves, peeled and crushed

red pepper, roasted until blackened, skinned, seeded and chopped

chilli, 1 red, chopped, with seeds

potato, large, 1, cut into 12mm (½") dice

sweet potato, ½, peeled, cut into 12mm (½") dice

fresh coriander, chopped, good handful

Cajun herb mill, 10 good twists

Noilly Prat, 1 slug

okra, 12, leave whole, just trim the stalks

lemon juice from 1 lemon

groundnut oil, 1 glug

salt to taste

For the stock:

the retained fish skin and prawn heads and shells

onion, ½, peeled and chopped

leek, ½, topped tailed and rough sliced

carrot, small, 1, rough chopped

bay leaves, 2

peppercorns, black, 5

water, 1 litre (2 pints), cold

6 portions

Tip – put the roasted peppers into a plastic freezer bag and seal for 5 minutes after removing from the oven; this will make them easier to peel

First, make the stock - put the prawn heads and shells and fish skin into a pan containing the cold water. Add the onion, leek, carrot, bay leaves, and peppercorns and bring to the boil. Simmer for around 45 minutes to 1 hour, then strain and set the liquor aside.

Chop the fish into bite-sized chunks while the stock is simmering.

Chop the onion and chilli and add to the oil which should be hot and fry gently until the onion is soft and translucent. Add the stock and roasted red pepper, potato, sweet potato, and Cajun spices and simmer, lid off, for around 1½ hours until well reduced. Then whizz with a hand blender, but not completely, to leave a chunky texture.

Add the fish and simmer for another 5 minutes before adding the prawns. After a couple of minutes add the scallops, okra, coriander, Noilly Prat and lemon juice and put the lid on the pan to help cook the okra, adding salt to taste. Simmer for 5 more minutes, then remove from the heat. Now you're ready to serve.

Variegated chillies, in the purple stage, growing at home

Spicy seafood chowder, a variation on a theme

cod fillet, 1, skin removed, but retained, chopped into bite sized pieces

ling fillet, 1, skin removed, but retained, chopped into bite sized pieces

king prawns, 8, uncooked, shells removed and retained, each cut into three pieces

white crab meat, 1½ handfuls (around 150g, or 6 oz)

watercress, 2 handfuls

coriander, fresh, chopped, including stalks, 1 good handful

new potatoes, 6, small, diced

onion, 1, chopped

garlic, 2 cloves, crushed

red chilli, chopped, with seeds

Noilly Prat, very good slug

Cajun spices

lemons, 2, juice of

For the stock

crab shell (not essential)

fish skins

prawn shells

onion, 1, peeled and chopped

carrot, 1 peeled and chopped

celery, 2 sticks, topped and tailed, chopped

black peppercorns, 6

bay leaves, 4

water, 1½ litres (3 pints)

6 Portions

First you need to make the stock. Nothing complicated – just put all the stock ingredients into a stockpot and bring to the boil. Turn down and simmer for 45 minutes. Sieve and retain the stock (there should be around 1 litre, 2 pints - exact amount doesn't matter), and throw away the bits.

Now add the stock to a large saucepan, add the Noilly Prat and bring to the boil then reduce to a simmer. After 30 minutes add the potatoes, and simmer for a further 30 minutes stirring occasionally. By now the stock should have thickened considerably.

Fry the onions, chilli and garlic till soft, add to the stock pot, then add the fish and prawns and after 10 minutes mash the fish pieces and prawns with the back of a wooden spoon, or a potato masher – not completely - to leave the fish and prawns in smaller pieces. Now add the Cajun spices and lemon juice. Simmer, stirring frequently now, for another 15 minutes, then add the coriander and crabmeat. Simmer for another 3 minutes.

Chilli flowers, on plants growing at home

SOUPS AND SALADS

Stock

Good stock is really easy to make and well worth the effort. It makes a great base for soups, and reduced it makes great sauces. My approach is to keep most of the basic ingredients the same for most flavours, fish, shellfish or fowl.

Basics:

carrots, 2, or 1 large, washed and rough chopped

bay leaves, 9, scrunched up in your hand to release flavours

black peppercorns, 11

large onion, 1 peeled and rough chopped

celery, 2 sticks, tops off, bottom rooty bits trimmed off, rough chopped

leek, 1, top and any bottom rooty bits trimmed off, cleaned, rough chopped.

You'll also need a 7 litre (14 pint) stockpot and a large saucepan or medium Le Creuset for fish if making a small amount. Use the stockpot if you've been hoarding a growing number of fish frames in the freezer – you'll always get more in the pot than you think, as the frames break up as they cook. Just a thought here – if you're lucky enough to be able to get large fish heads from the fishmonger, try just poaching them in the stock mix for 7 minutes, removing them and then picking off the head meat then putting back the bones. You might be surprised how much meat there is, and it's great for fishcakes!

Flavours:

Fish, and crab are my favourites. Chicken, duck, pheasant, guinea fowl, and turkey are good too, and so are the woody ends of asparagus, for an asparagus soup base, which is a little different.

Use the shells from crab, lobster and prawns, and the frames, (bones and skin) from fresh fish, for stock for seafood and fish soups and sauces. If you're buying fish from a fishmonger ask for the frames if you're buying fillets, and leave them in the freezer until you're ready to make the stock. Use the bones and carcases from roast chicken, duck, pheasant, partridge and guinea fowl to make stock for vegetable and poultry based soups and sauces.

Put the flavouring into the stockpot, followed by the basics, then top up with water to 25mm – 50mm (1" - 2") below top of stockpot. Use the lid to manage the rate of liquor evaporation, leaving it off if it is going too slowly, putting it on and leaving a gap if it is going too quickly.

Simmer crab and lobster stocks for 1 hour and fish for 45 minutes. For poultry and game bird stocks bring to the boil and simmer without lid for 2 hours. Use the lid to regulate the rate of evaporation if you like (more open = less reduction, more closed = more reduction), but with fish be careful as if it is too closed the stock may boil over.

For asparagus, save the woody bits in a bag in the freezer when you've prepped the asparagus for cooking until you've two or ideally 3 or 4 bundlesworths. Add 1 litre (2 pints) of water to a pan, then simply add the woody bits sliced in half lengthways and half an onion, chopped, bring to the boil and simmer for 2 hours, topping up with water every 40 minutes.

Strain the liquor and bones/shell/skin/vegetables through a colander, pressing down (using a hand is easiest) on the mush to extract ALL the juice.

You've now got the base for loads of soups. It freezes well. And the Basics, plus a couple of tomatoes (left overs from Barcelona breakfast, see page 106 in Early Bird) make a really tasty vegetable stock.

Asparagus soup, with poached eggs and crispy pancetta

The pancetta is especially for my sister Lucia who adores this soup.

asparagus ends – from snapping the stalks - ideally 18 or more, sliced in half lengthways

shallot, 2, peeled and fine chopped (small onions are fine if you don't have shallots)

goats' butter, 2 knobs

vegetable oil, ½ glug

asparagus spears, medium or thick, 3 or 4 per person, woody ends removed as above, chopped into 12mm (½") pieces

mushrooms, button, ideally chestnut, medium, 4, sliced

eggs, 4

white wine vinegar, 1 tablespoon

pancetta, 2 slices, fried until crispy, then broken into medium squares, (optional) If you don't want to use the pancetta try grating a little Parmesan or Pecorino (ewes' milk) over the soup at the end.

2 portions, wonderful for breakfast – ideally make stock the night before; it takes an hour at least.

Put asparagus ends and 1 shallot into 1 litre (2 pints) of water, simmer at least 1 hour, ideally 2, top up occasionally with more water to stop drying out. Strain the stock into a bowl then squeeze the asparagus and shallot into the bowl to extract all their juices.

Heat medium pan over medium heat, add 1 knob of goats' butter, and when melted add the other shallot. Fry gently for 5 minutes then add HALF the asparagus. Fry for 10 minutes, add the stock to the pan, bring to the boil, simmer for 30 minutes. While this is happening, melt the last of the goats' butter in a small pan, and when hot add the mushrooms. Fry and turn for 10 minutes, remove, and dry on kitchen towel.

When the soup has had 30 minutes, blitz with a blender, add the rest of the asparagus and the mushrooms, and simmer for 6 minutes. Have a kettle of boiling water to hand.

Serve the soup into preheated bowls. Add recently boiled water to the soup pan, return to the boil, add the vinegar, carefully break the eggs into the water and poach gently FOR 1 MINUTE. When whites are still translucent lift the eggs out carefully, and float onto the soup. Sprinkle with the pancetta, if using, and serve.

Fantastic way to use up all those asparagus ends

Butter bean and garlic salad

butter beans, 1 tin, good quality (400g, 1lb), drained

garlic, 4 cloves, peeled and finely chopped

white wine vinegar, 1 glug

very good olive oil, 2 good glugs

2 – 4 portions depending how much you and your friends like garlic!

Put the beans onto a plate with edges, or a very shallow dish, sprinkle the garlic over, then add the vinegar and oil. Mix well to ensure the garlic is evenly spread, and the oil and vinegar are coating the beans well.

This will take around 1 hour to marinade, when all the flavours are well mixed. Go back to the mixture every 10 minutes and give a stir, and to spoon the liquor over the beans.

Chestnut mushroom salad

chestnut button mushrooms, 12, finely sliced

balsamic vinegar, a light sprinkling (½ a glug)

good olive oil, 1 glug

toasted sesame oil, a light sprinkling (½ a glug)

salt, 1 pinch

4 portions

Again, very easy to make, and an interesting sideshow to the main salad event, adding variety and flavours to the meal.

Simply place the mushrooms on a shallow dish, sprinkle the balsamic, toasted sesame and olive oils over and toss, then sprinkle on the salt. Fantastic combination of flavours in this one and so easy to make. Best eaten after leaving to meld for an hour or so.

Courgette, rocket and tomato soup

vegetable stock, good, 1½ litres (3 pints)

woody asparagus ends, 2 handfuls (around 18)

rocket, loads, stalks and all (use 2 packets if from the supermarket)

medium onion, 1, peeled and chopped

courgettes, 3 large or 6 small, topped and tailed, medium sliced

tomatoes, large, 6, chopped and woody bits removed

groundnut oil, 1 glug

salt, 2 teaspoons or more to taste

white pepper, 2 teaspoons or more to taste

6 portions

Make up the stock, being wary of shop bought in case of gluten or yeast extract if you don't have home-made (follow my stock recipe on page 57 in *Soups and Salads* to see how), bring to the boil and then add the rocket and asparagus. Simmer for 1 hour until reduced by around one third and the rocket and asparagus flavours have been passed into the stock.

Strain to remove the bits, discard and set the stock aside.

Heat a soup pan over medium heat, and when hot add the oil, closely followed by the onion. Fry lightly until soft and translucent (taking around 5 minutes), then add the courgettes and tomatoes.

Fry for 5 minutes, add the strained stock, white pepper and salt. Simmer for half an hour then blitz with a blender. Continue cooking for half an hour to an hour, reducing the soup quite a lot and really concentrating the flavours, turning the reduction into a delicious creamy soup.

While reducing, taste occasionally to see if you want to add more pepper or salt, and to help you decide when to take it off the heat.

This soup is great **hot or cold**, winter or summer – take your pick.

Crab tomato and coriander soup

crab stock, 3 litres (6 pints). Go to page 58 for my stock recipe in *Soups and Salads* to see method

onion, medium, 1, peeled and chopped

goats' butter, 1 knob

tomatoes, large, ripe, 6, skinned and chopped (to remove skin blanch for 2 minutes then peel

salt, good pinch

coriander, fresh, large bunch, tied with string

bread, fresh, 1 slice per portion, toasted or fried depending on your taste, for croutons. You can use my Soda bread recipe on page 127. It works really well for croutons.

garlic, 1 clove, peeled

6 portions

Reduce the stock to 1½ litres (3 pints) by simmering for around one hour.

Gently fry the onion in melted goats' butter until soft and translucent (around 5 minutes), then add the tomatoes. Simmer gently for 10 minutes, stir frequently, add salt.

Now add the stock and the coriander and simmer for one hour, which will reduce the soup and thicken it. Remove from the heat and remove the coriander, squeezing it carefully to extract all the juices, then whizz with a blender.

Rub the garlic over the toasted or fried bread, cut into croutons and place in the soup bowls, then ladle the soup on top.

This soup can be quite filling, so leave room for a second helping rather than overdo the first.

Crab and watercress soup

crab stock, 1 litre (2 pints), following my recipe on page 58 in *Soups and Salads* to see method

onion, medium, 1, peeled and chopped

watercress, 2 packets equivalent, stalks and all, rough chopped

groundnut oil, 1 glug

2 - 4 portions, depending how hungry you are

Heat oil in saucepan over medium heat and when hot add onion and gently fry until soft and translucent (takes around 5 minutes). Add the stock, bring to boil and simmer for 15 minutes.

Add ¾ of the watercress and simmer, lid off for another 45 minutes, then blitz with a blender. The flavours should have intensified by now but better test the taste and if you want more flavour, carry on reducing until you're happy.

When you're ready, ladle the soup into bowls and garnish with the rest of the watercress before serving.

Fish soup, Eastern style with coriander

fish / seafood stock, strong, 1½ litres (3 pints), following my recipe on page 58 in *Soups and Salads* to see method

onion, medium, 1, peeled and chopped

red chillies, ½, with seeds if you like it hot, chopped

garlic, 1 clove, peeled and chopped

coriander, fresh, with stalks, 1 good handful

toasted sesame oil, 2 good glugs

lemon, ½, juice of

2 portions

As it stands, this is a lovely light soup and makes a great starter. If you want something a bit more substantial just add a few chunks of cod, monkfish, or haddock and a handful of prawns around 10 minutes before the end.

Put the soup pan over a medium heat and when hot, add the toasted sesame oil. When the oil is hot, add the onions chillies and garlic. Fry until the onions are soft and translucent (around 5 minutes), stirring occasionally, then add the stock and simmer gently until reduced by half. Almost ready to serve now - just add the coriander and blitz with a blender, then add the lemon juice. Just give your soup a stir, and you're ready to go. . . . .

Unless you want to add the additional Eastern authenticity mentioned overleaf . . . .

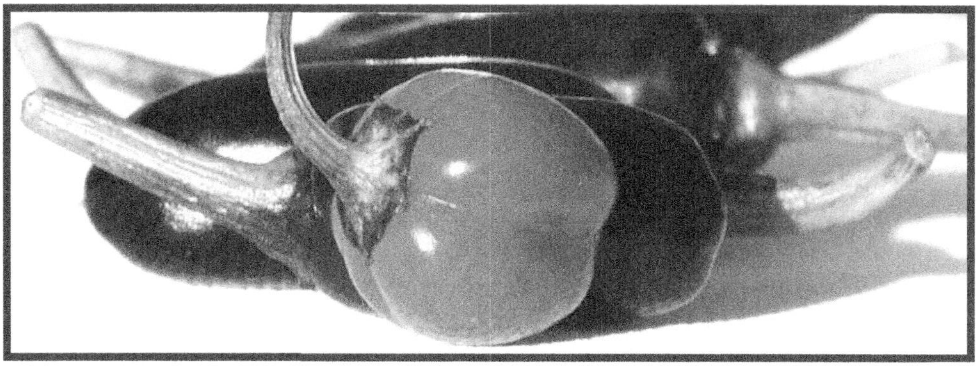

Chillies grown at home

For Eastern style spiciness, dried or fresh lime or lemon leaves if you can get them add a touch of authenticity, along with ginger, chilli and fresh coriander. Feel free to add ginger to this recipe too if you like as well as fresh lime or lemon leaves.

SAUCES AND SIDES

Bean meze

flageolet beans, 1 tin (400g, 1lb), drained and dried

garlic, 3 cloves, peeled, crushed

onion, medium, 1, peeled and fine chopped

good olive oil, 4 good glugs

parsley, including stalks, chopped, 2 good handfuls

salt, 2 good pinches

2 portions

This dish is great on its own with bread or as a dip for raw vegetables.

First put a wok over a medium heat, and when warm, add the oil. Don't get the oil too hot, because now you're going to add the parsley, and fry gently if you can – it might spitter and spatter a bit, and after 2 minutes add the garlic and onions, continue frying gently. You don't want to fry this too quickly as you're getting the flavours of the parsley, garlic and onion infused in the oil.

After 10 minutes add the beans, turn up the heat and fry for a further 15 minutes, stirring occasionally. You're going to continue cooking until the beans are soft enough to mash with the back of a wooden spoon. So, let 15 minutes go by and now experiment and see if the beans are squishable. Squish away for 5 minutes, stirring as you go. After another 10 minutes the beans will be very soft so squish again, using the potato masher if it is hard going with the back of the spoon.

You should end up with the mush being the consistency of thick yoghurt with small chunks of fruit, so when ready, just serve. You could also try it cold, on toast, as a snack.

Beetroot marmalade

beetroot, fresh, small - medium, 4, cooked, small diced

shallot, 2, peeled and sliced, pushed out into rings

good olive oil, 1 glug

vegetable stock, 125ml (1/4 pint)

salt to taste

if you'd like this spicy, try adding a ½ teaspoon of chopped chilli at the beginning with the shallot

2 portions

This dish is so easy to make and a great accompaniment to cheese or a salad.

Simply heat the oil in a small saucepan, on a low light, and then add the shallot. You are going to caramelise it very slowly, so you only need a low light, and it will take around 30 minutes. You're looking for the shallot to cook in its own juices, becoming very, very soft.

When caramelisation has happened add the beetroot, stirring it in, add the stock, and leave on the low light for around 30 - 40 minutes until the mixture has reduced to a 'sauce' consistency, Then see if the beetroot is soft enough to squish with the edge of a wooden spoon. If so, squish around ¾ of the pieces, while leaving the pan on the stove. If the mixture looks a little dry, add a little more groundnut oil. Keep on reducing until it is the right consistency.

The marmalade is finished when most of the beetroot has been squished. If you're labouring with the edge of a spoon, try the potato masher, gently pressing and turning it onto the mixture until you have the right consistency.

The intriguing St Michael's Mount at Marazion

Broccoli, spicy stir-fried

broccoli, 1 head including stalks, chopped into small bite-sized pieces

vegetable oil, 1 splash

sesame oil, 1 splash

red chilli, no seeds, finely chopped

garlic, 2 cloves, peeled, finely chopped

tamari soy, 5 splashes

portions, probably 2, maybe more but this is delicious cold and can be eaten as a salad.

This is another really easy dish to make, and does not take long to prepare or cook.

Get a medium sized or large saucepan hot. You don't need a wok but if you've got one feel free to use it. Add the oils and when hot add all the ingredients EXCEPT the soy. Stir-fry for 5 minutes, add the soy, stir fry for a further 5 minutes and it's good to go

Cauliflower with mustard seeds and turmeric

cauliflower florets, small – medium, 15

yellow or black mustard seeds, 3 teaspoons

goats' butter, 1 knob

salt, 1 pinch

turmeric, 2 teaspoons

2 portions

This dish takes around 15 minutes from start to finish, so time it to coincide with whatever else you're having. It's a small dish, a great accompaniment to a curry, and it's not half bad cold as a snack!

You'll need a medium sized saucepan with a tight-fitting lid for this because it is actually the steam generated by the hot cauliflower that cooks the cauliflower. If the lid isn't tight fitting, the steam will escape and you'll end up with everything very dry and stuck to the bottom of the pan.

Place the pan over a medium heat and when hot add the goats' butter. When the goats' butter has melted add the mustard seeds and put the lid on. After a couple of minutes the seeds will start to pop (if the lid isn't on they'll be jumping out all over the place). A minute after the seeds have begun to pop, lift the lid quickly and give a stir then replace the lid. When the seeds have stopped popping, which will be after another minute or so, add the turmeric and stir, then add the cauliflower and stir until all the florets are coated in the glorious yellow mixture, and put the lid back on.

Now turn the heat down a little and simply allow the cauliflower to cook away for around 10 minutes. Half way through you can take a peak if you like and give a stir just to make absolutely sure that nothing is burning or sticking – I'm always amazed that it just doesn't. Shake the pan occasionally too if you're worried.

Now serve. The combination of the distinctive taste of the turmeric with the sweetness of the cauliflower really makes this dish.

Cod paste, Italian style

cod fillet, 1

garlic, 1 clove

good olive oil, 3 glugs

2 portions

I got this idea from visiting my sister Lucia who lives half of her life in Milan. It is a popular Italian café breakfast snack in some parts, spread on bread, washed down with a glass or two of red wine. I tried it and loved it so decided to recreate in Cornwall.

First salt the cod by covering the fillet with sea salt and leaving for a couple of hours, then wash off the salt under a cold tap and dry the fillet with kitchen towel. Don't leave the salt on for longer because too much will be absorbed, making the fish too salty and spoiling the flavour.

Skin the cod and chop into bite-sized pieces. Heat a frying pan over a medium heat and when warm add the oil. When the oil is warm add the garlic and fry gently. You're just wanting to flavour the oil rather than fry the garlic so continue to fry very gently for around 10 minutes stirring frequently before adding the cod and continuing to fry gently for around 30 more minutes, by which time the oil should have been reduced somewhat.

Now put all in a blender, blitz for 10 - 15 seconds and the paste will be ready. Remove from the blender, put in a small bowl and allow to cool.

This cod paste is delicious spread on rolls, flat bread, or hot or cold toast, for breakfast, or just as a light snack.

For something similar, and equally easy and surprising, try my seafood paste, Italian style in Sauces and Sides on page 88.

Courgette marmalade

courgettes, medium, 2, topped and tailed, cut into matchsticks

shallot, 1, peeled and sliced and pushed out into rings

good olive oil, 1 glug

vegetable stock, 125ml (¼ pint)

salt to taste

if you'd like this spicy, try adding a ½ teaspoon of chopped chilli at the beginning with the shallot.

2 portions

This is another great accompaniment to cheese and salads and the preparation is virtually identical to the beetroot marmalade. In fact, the only difference is that the courgettes are not pre-cooked.

So, heat the oil on a very low light, then add the shallot, stirring occasionally until well caramelised – which will take about 30 minutes. Then add the courgettes and stock, and again stir occasionally, for around 30 - 40 minutes. When the courgette is sufficiently soft, squish it, using the edge of a wooden spoon or a potato masher.

Critters

For this great recipe, which is my absolute favourite of all time, using courgettes and fresh garden mint, see And Finally, on page 129.

Mashed potato and flavourings

I like to use a potato ricer for mashing potato, sometimes I crush them using the back of a fork, so if you don't have a ricer, just carry on with a fork. I find it much easier than most mashers!

Boil medium sized potatoes, unpeeled, fairly vigorously, whole until soft enough to mash (15 – 20 minutes should do it; you should be able to push a fork into them, but not too easily). Drain and leave in pan until dried from heat of the pan (1 – 2 minutes). Put each potato into a ricer whole and still unpeeled, and over a bowl squeeze the top handle down towards the bottom handle, pressing the potato through the mesh in the bottom of the ricer, picture below.

The skin will be left in the ricer and you will get fluffy dry potato in the bowl. Add a big knob of butter or extra virgin olive oil or cold pressed rapeseed oil, and mix lightly with a fork until evenly spread through, then add milk or cream, salt, and white pepper to taste.

You can prepare the mash before the other things you're cooking and heat it up for a couple of minutes in the microwave when you're ready to serve; then you don't have to worry so much about timing.

Different flavours can be added to the mash to complement the potato flavour, and what you add will depend on the meal you're preparing. My favourites, all made with a handful or two of fresh leaves, include tarragon, coriander, chive, coriander and chive, parsley, watercress, and mint. Additionally, English mustard mash is great with meats and roasted tomato mash with fish. Most go well with either meats or fish, but mustard mash is especially good with beef, roasted tomato mash with fish, and parsley mash with fish too.

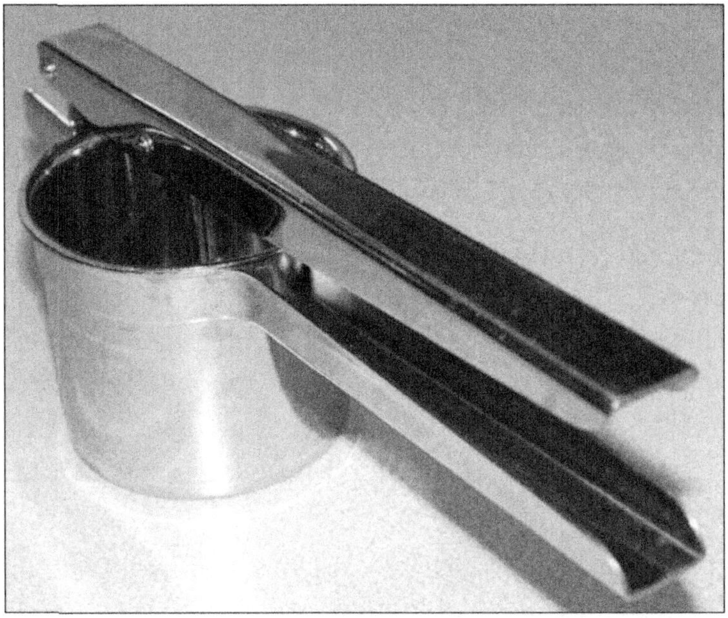

Potato ricer

Beautifully fluffy riced potato, ready for mashing

Mushy Peas

marrowfat peas, dried, 1 packet (250g or 10oz), soaked for 12 hours and rinsed in cold water. NOT the quick soak type.

onion, 1, peeled and finely chopped

garlic cloves, 2, peeled, whole

thyme, fresh, 4 – 5 stalks, whole, around 10cm (4") long

goats' butter, around 50g (2oz)

water, 1½ - 2 litres (3 – 4 pints)

salt to taste

white pepper to taste

water, to cover peas as they cook

6 – 8 portions, but it does depend on what you do with them. They freeze well.

Patience is needed, and timing can be a little difficult but the result is well worth the effort. A great accompaniment to fish; poached, fried or grilled, or in fish pasties of pea and cheese bites.

Once the peas are ready, best soaked overnight, follow the instructions on the packet, add them to a large saucepan and cover them by about 25mm (1") of cold water. Add the onion, garlic and thyme, and bring to the boil. Turn down, bring to a simmer and simmer gently for around ¾ hour to 1 hour.

You will need to stir the pan every 10 minutes or so to stop the bottom peas burning, and for the last 20 minutes it is best to keep a close eye on the peas, stirring every 5 minutes as they can over-thicken very quickly if you're not careful. If it looks as though the peas are not yet cooked but there is too little moisture left, just add a bit more water.

The idea here is to cook it slow and long, until the peas are mushy, by which time the onion, garlic and thyme will have been dissolved and be part of the overall glorious flavour. The thyme sprigs will need taking out before serving if you can find them – if not just warn your guests to look out for them.

When the peas are slightly more liquid than the consistency you are looking to end up with, remove from the heat and add the goats' butter, stirring it in until dissolved, which will thicken the peas further. Ideally some of the peas will still be whole, suspended in a fantastic thick sauce.

When cool, the mushy peas turn a rather dull grey colour. Don't worry, they still taste wonderful and heat up well in a pan over a low light with a little more water added to maintain consistency.

They really make my fish pasty (recipe on page 28), and are brilliantly melded with hard goats' or sheeps' cheese in my mushy pea and cheese bites (recipe on page 35).

Plum and parsley chutney

Another fruity flavour great with mackerel

shallots, 2, peeled and chopped

good olive oil, 2 good slugs

vegetable stock, 125ml (¼ pint)

plums, ripe, 10, skinned, stones removed, chopped

parsley, leaves only, 1 handful

Marsala, 1 slug

2 portions

This is another chutney that is great with cheeses.

First caramelise the shallots by putting the oil over a low light until warm and then adding the shallot and stirring. It will take quite a while, 30 minutes or so, to caramelise them when they'll be really sweet and a very dark brown.

Then, add the Marsala, vegetable stock, plums and parsley. Simmer for around 45 minutes to 1 hour, stirring occasionally until the mixture is well reduced and you can mash the plums with the back of a fork, wooden spoon or potato masher. As with the other sauces and chutneys similar to this one, you're looking to keep on the heat until the chutney is the consistency of a thick chunky soup, which will thicken more as it cools.

Then take off the heat and wait to cool, spoon into a small serving bowl and take to the table to enjoy with your cheeses.

Plumptious plum sauce

plums, 450 gm, 1lb, destoned, roughly sliced

red chilli, 1, deseeded, finely chopped

caster sugar, 75gm, just under 3oz

white wine vinegar, 100ml, just under 1/5 pint

water, 150ml, ¼ pint

ginger, fresh, grated, 1 teaspoon

soy sauce, 1 teaspoon

salt, to taste, about ½ teaspoon

Sichuan peppercorns, 7

This is really easy. Just add all ingredients to a medium sized saucepan, bring to the boil and simmer for one hour, stirring occasionally and mashing the mixture with the back of a fork every 10 minutes or so to break up the plums.

Remove the Sichuan peppercorns and allow to cool a little before pouring this delicious chutney into a bowl.

I especially enjoy it with grilled mackerel, and with a wide range of cheeses.

Rhubarb relish

shallots, 2, peeled and chopped

good olive oil, 2 good slugs

vegetable stock, 125ml (1/4 pint)

rhubarb, 2 sticks, topped and tailed, cut into matchsticks

Marsala, 1 slug

2 portions

This relish is great, along with the others, with cheeses. Because it is different, it is well worth the effort to make it to see what you think of it.

First you need to caramelise the shallots – heat the oil over a low light until warm and then put the shallots in and stir. It will take quite a while, 30 minutes or so, to caramelise them when they will be really sweet and very dark brown. You can pretty much leave them to their own devices as long as the light is very low because they will not burn. If the heat is too high you'll need to be there to stir, and they'll be ready more quickly but not as soft and sweet.

Then add the Marsala, vegetable stock, and rhubarb and, simmer for around 45 minutes to 1 hour, stirring occasionally until the mixture is well reduced and you can mash the rhubarb with the back of a fork, wooden spoon, or potato masher. You're looking to keep on the heat until the relish is the consistency of a thick chunky soup, which will thicken more as it cools.

Allow to cool and serve. Also brilliant with grilled mackerel.

Saffron milk sauce for poaching fish or pouring

goats' or plant-based milk, whole, 1 pint

onion, small, ½, peeled and finely chopped

goats' butter, 1 very generous knob (around 50 grams or 2 ounces should be fine)

saffron, 1 very good pinch

gluten free plain flour, 1 teaspoon

2 portions

This is a brilliant sauce for fish. You can poach fish in it, or just make it separately to pour over fish when cooked differently.

Slowly melt goats' butter in a large pan then add the onion, frying gently until soft and translucent (around 5 minutes). Add the goats' or plant-based milk and saffron; bring to slow simmer and at this point add your fish if you are using the sauce for poaching.

If poaching, cover pan and gently poach fish for 6 minutes. Gently remove fish, drain it into pan, place in cold water to stop it cooking, and set aside to warm through again later.

Put the gluten free plain flour in mug, add 2 teaspoons of water, stir until you have made a thick paste.

Continue to simmer liquor until reduced to around one third of original volume and the saffron has given it a beautiful golden yellow tint, then add the gluten free plain flour paste and stir continuously to stop it going lumpy, until sauce has thickened, when it will be ready.

Either pour over the cooked, and reheated if necessary, fish before taking the plates to the table or, better still, put it into a warmed white jug which will set off the beautifully coloured sauce and take this to the table for people to help themselves.

Seafood paste, Italian style

scallops, 6, with coral

prawns, cooked, 12, small, bought shell on, heads and shells removed

garlic, ½ clove, peeled and sliced

good olive oil, 3 good glugs

coriander, fresh, rough chopped, with stalks, 1 handful

2 portions

First you're going to flavour the oil with the coriander and garlic to get a melded taste rather than individual flavours; take a bowl and put the oil, garlic and coriander in it, stir well, then put cling over and leave to meld overnight in the fridge, or for at least 4 – 5 hours. Stir occasionally, and before use, remove the coriander and garlic from the oil by straining well.

Take a wok or medium sized saucepan and place over a medium heat; when hot add the oil and get it sizzling, then add the scallops and prawns. Stir well, crush every few minutes with the back of a fork and reduce until the mixture is quite thick. This will take around 30 minutes.

Put all the ingredients into a blender and blitz. You'll end up with a beautifully orange paste which you should remove from the blender, put in a small bowl and allow to cool.

Spread the seafood paste on hot toast or flat bread or serve as a dip with raw vegetables.

Goes well alongside the intriguing and delicious Cod Paste, Italian style. My recipe is on page 76.

Splotties

Splotties are a great way of using up the mashed potato or squished potato not served from the previous night, for breakfast, whether flavoured or plain – a good excuse for making too much for dinner!

portions - mashed or squished potato sufficient for 1 person at a normal serving provides enough for 2 splotties, which are a bit like potato cakes.

You will also need a knob of goats' butter and an egg.

Simply put the potato into a mixing bowl and beat in a whole egg, until the mixture has lightened and is quite gooey. Heat a frying pan, until quite hot, then add goats' butter, and when sizzling, using a large serving spoon, scoop out a heaped spoonful of the splotty mix and dollop it sharply into the pan, and then repeat until the mix is all gone or the pan is fully loaded.

Allow to sizzle for 2 – 3 minutes, gently nudging the splotties around the pan to make sure they don't stick. Then turn them, and you will see they have turned golden brown on the cooked side.

Leave for another 2 – 3 minutes and remove from the pan. Keep warm in the oven while you cook the eggs.

Or try adding chopped tomato, chopped soft herbs such as tarragon or chervil or flaked smoked mackerel, stirring into the splotty mix with a tablespoon of double goats' or plant-based cream before cooking, then serve with poached eggs.

FROM THE GRILL

Christmas Eve barbequed sea bass with vanilla, tomato and basil

The Treloar family members who are not strictly vegetarian, and friends and relatives visiting Cove Farm for the festivities, always eat fish on Christmas Eve and whenever the weather permits – and that means when it isn't actually pouring with rain or snowing - this is what we have.

sea bass, 1, gutted, scaled

plum tomatoes, 3

thin slices of goats' butter, 4

vanilla pods, 2

basil leaves, large, 4 (or small – supermarket size - 10)

string – 600mm (2ft)

2 portions

"WHAT!!" I can hear you say – "BARBEQUING BASS?........AT THAT PRICE!!" Believe me it is well worth experimenting with this dish. This is quite different from cooking bass in the oven or the frying pan; it is a lovely dish that is fairly easy to prepare and cook, and to watch as the skin crisps and browns over the hot coals.

First deepen the cavity; hold the fish so the cavity is at the top and use a large knife to cut downwards towards the back and backwards towards the tail. Then, slice the tomatoes, removing the woody bits. Now take the vanilla pods and slice them in half lengthways and use the knife blade to scrape along the pods to remove the seeds. Spread the seeds on one side of the tomatoes, then place a layer of tomatoes inside the cavity, then a layer of basil leaves then a slice of goats' butter. Repeat the layering until the tomatoes basil and goats' butter are used up.

Now tie one end of the string around the fish, knotting tightly before winding the string round and round to close the cavity before tying it off.

Place over hot coals, with the cavity angled upwards to prevent the succulent juices dripping out and cook for just 4 minutes per side.

Make sure the coals are really hot and DON'T overcook this wonderful fish.

The meat is fairly soft so carve the fillets carefully and serve with the tomatoes and leaves, which will have a delicious hint of vanilla.

Courgette (blackened) and roquefort sandwiches, barbequed

courgettes, 2, medium

Roquefort, goats' or other soft sheeps' cheese, fresh, 6 tablespoons

balsamic vinegar, 2 glugs

salt, 2 – 3 pinches to taste

good olive oil, 2 good glugs

2 portions

While this is a great dish to eat outside as a course of a barbeque meal you can always use a hot oven instead. If you've got friends round, they'll think you're very creative, especially if you do use the barbeque, but it's really simple to make.

First, slice the courgettes, lengthways into medium slices around 6mm (¼") thick, sprinkle the oil over and rub to make sure all surfaces are covered, then put on the barbeque grill. Turn every three or four minutes and cook until the courgettes are beginning to blacken, which should take around 10 minutes depending on how hot the coals are. Remove from the grill and place onto a board and sprinkle with balsamic and salt, then spread the roquefort on one side of each slice of courgettes apart from the top one and rebuild the slices into 2 tall courgettes.

Now place the re-assembled courgettes on 2 pieces of kitchen foil and wrap into parcels. Place on the grill for around 15 more minutes and you're ready to go. The sweetness of the melted goats' or sheeps' cheese complements the hint of harshness of the slightly charred courgette..

Mackerel, plain grilled on the barbeque

Mackerel fillets, 2 medium or one large per person

Vegetable oil

portions, as many as you like!

Wipe the clean grill using a piece of kitchen towel dipped in vegetable oil which will help to stop the fillets stocking to it. Then simply brush the mackerel fillets with vegetable oil on the skin side and lay, skin side down, gently on the grill which should be around 150mm (6") above the coals which should be very hot.

Leave for five to six minutes, but keep an eye on them. If the oil from the fish drips to the coals and begins catching fire and flaring, gently move the fillets to another spot over the coals to avoid them becoming burnt or sooty.

To cook on an indoor grill simply turn the grill to high, place the fillets skin side up onto a piece of oiled kitchen foil on the grill tray, not too close to the grill itself – try the 2nd shelf down, brush with vegetable oil and leave under the grill for 5 – 6 minutes.

The skin will be lovely and crispy so serve the fillets skin side up to keep it that way.

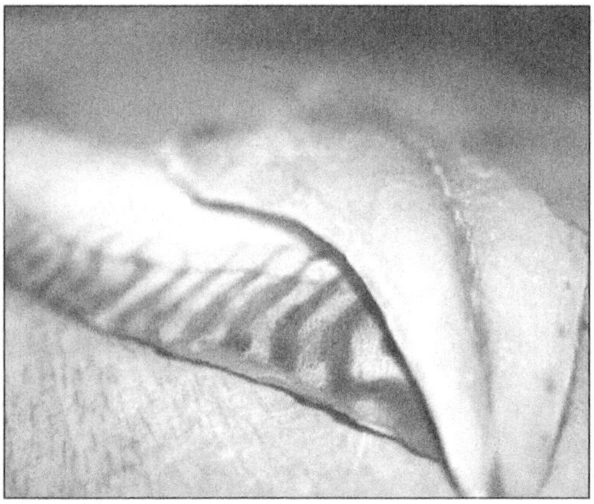

Fresh mackerel fillets, ideal for the barbeque or indoor grill.

Mackerel, stuffed with orange and fennel, on the barbeque

mackerel, 2 large, guts removed, rinsed and dried inside and out

orange, 1, sliced

fennel, 1 very thin sliced

2 portions

The orange and fennel really cut through the oiliness of the mackerel and the combination of flavours is superb.

Expand the cavity of the mackerel using a sharp knife, then simply put the fennel and orange in layers inside each fish. Use string to tie the mackerel so the cavity is more or less closed. Leave to marinade for an hour or so before putting on a grill over hot coals.

When placing the mackerel, lay them so the cavities are angled slightly upwards – this will ensure that most of the juices stay inside the fish rather than drain out onto the coals. Turn after 5 minutes, leave for another 5 minutes then remove from the grill.

Untie the fish, remove the orange and fennel, and serve on plates with the orange and fennel arranged at the side of the mackerel............delicious.

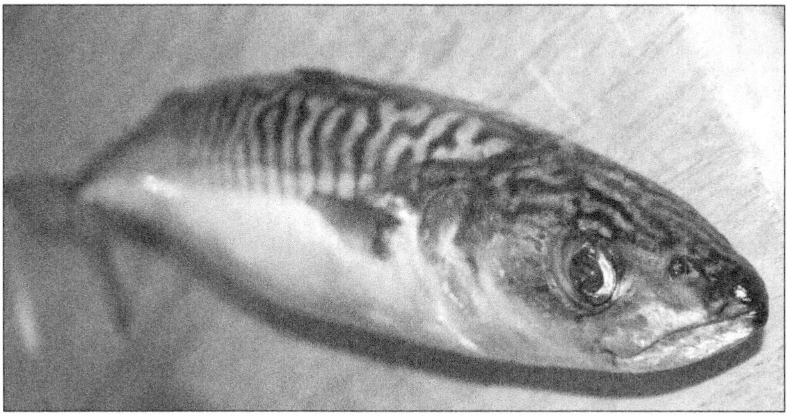

Simple to prepare and easy cooking on the barbeque

Mushrooms, large, marinated and barbequed

This is great with plain grilled or barbequed white fish or as a starter

large flat or Portobello mushrooms, 4, stalks removed

groundnut oil, 3 good glugs

goats' butter, 1 knob

For the marinade

good olive oil, 3 good glugs

juice – from ½ lemon, or orange – try 2 different batches, one of each

good white wine, 1 slug

garlic, 1 clove, peeled and crushed

salt, good pinch

2 per person makes a great BBQ starter

First put all the marinade ingredients into a bowl, mix together then leave for 30 minutes to allow the flavours to meld.

While the marinade is melding clean the mushrooms and remove the stalks, place the mushrooms in a baking tray or large shallow dish. When the marinade is ready, pour it into the upturned mushrooms and leave for 45 minutes. The marinade will gradually be absorbed and after 45 minutes you may not see any of it. If there is some left, leave it there!

It is best not to leave the mushrooms marinading for longer than 45 minutes if you can avoid it otherwise they will take on the flavour of the marinade completely and you'll lose the mushroom taste in the cooked dish.

Brush the underside of the mushrooms with groundnut oil then put them onto the grill, upturned, over hot coals, with the grill 200mm – 225mm (8" - 9") above them, and after around 15 minutes the marinade should have reappeared and be bubbling gently, which is exactly what you want. Cooking for a further 5 minutes.

Then, carefully pour the liquor from each mushroom into a bowl or jug, turn them all over and put them back on the grill; brush what was the underside with the liquor. After 5 minutes turn them all again, pour a little of the liquor back into each mushroom. Then add a mini-knob of goats' butter to each mushroom, rubbing it over as the knob melts and cook for another 5 – 10 minutes and serve, still upturned, liquor still there.

Mushrooms barbequed, with Cornish Polmarkyn blue or white goats' cheese

For a different flavour, vary this marinated mushroom recipe slightly; after re-turning the mushrooms do not put any liquor back, but add Polmarkyn white or blue cheese. Polmarkyn Cornish cheese is fantastic but other English or French soft goats' cheese, or sheeps' cheese such as Roquefort, will also do well. Put a couple of thin slices in the centre of each mushroom, on top of the melted goats' butter, and when the cheese has melted spread it round each mushroom using a knife and serve immediately.

Scallops, shell poached on the barbeque, with ginger and soy sauce, topped with crumbled Parma ham

Again, this is great without the Parma ham if you don't eat meat

Parma ham, 4 slices, grilled and crumbled (optional)

garlic, 1 clove, finely chopped

fresh ginger, 1 generous thumbnail, finely chopped

good olive oil, 2 glugs

water, ½ cup

scallops, 6, with 12 shells

rice vinegar, 2 tablespoons

goats' butter, 2 knobs

2 starter portions

This can be prepared in advance of your barbeque, and is a fantastic way of showing off your BBQ flair and imagination. It can of course also be done using the oven to cook, but on the barbeque grill the look of the scallop shells and the aromas are just amazing.

Scallop shells. Just ask your fishmonger for them.

Heat a pan over a medium heat and when hot add the oil, then the garlic and ginger. The idea here is to create a spicy liquor, with the oil picking up the garlic and ginger flavours. So gently fry for around 15 minutes, adding the water, rice vinegar and goats' butter after 12 minutes.

Place the scallops in the shells and pour the liquor over, then place the remaining shells on top to cover. Place on a very hot grill (or in a hot oven), and cook or 5 minutes. Take to the table, remove the top shells and sprinkle with the Parma ham. Fantastic tastes and aromas!!

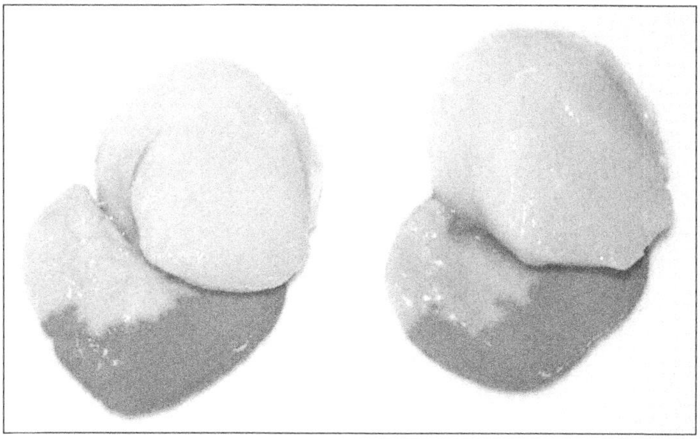

Beautiful scallops, complete with their delicious corals

EARLY BIRD

Barcelona breakfast

toast, 2 slices per person, cold

fresh tomatoes, medium, 1½ per person, halved

garlic, 1 large clove, peeled and halved

extra virgin olive oil, around 1 teaspoon per slice of toast, to drizzle when ready

Manchego cheese, sliced using potato peeler, enough to sprinkle over each slice

Fresh wild garlic if you can find it when in season (November to May in the right parts of Cornwall!), including flowers when they arrive, chopped, to sprinkle of top of each slice

sea salt, to taste

Mamá calls this pan con tomate, or sometimes Catalan bread. We all love it!

Rub the chopped edge of a piece of garlic over each side of each piece of toast. If someone prefers their garlic in low doses, rub only one side, as sparingly as you think necessary. Then squeeze the tomatoes over the top of each side of toast, 1½ tomatoes per 2 slices of toast, and spread the squeezed flesh as evenly as you can across each piece.

Then sprinkle the salt to taste, rubbing between thumb and fingers to crumble it, across each piece, and then drizzle olive oil over. I pour from the bottle usually, using my thumb to stop it gushing. Now sprinkle the cheese over, and finally the wild garlic, adding three or four flowers per piece of toast when they're in season.

Don't throw the tomato husks away. I use them chopped in sauces, stews, curries, chillies, pasta sauces and finely chopped in egg mayonnaise, my brother Flip's teatime treat.

Bubble & squeak omelette

eggs, 2

salt, 1 pinch

cabbage, cooked, (boiled for 10 – 15 minutes), drained and squeezed dry, teased apart, 3 tablespoons

mashed potato, 3 tablespoons

goats' butter, 1 knob

1 portion, double up for 2 omelettes but cook separately

Weird but wonderful....................it can be really surprising what you can do with leftovers, and this is certainly no exception. I wouldn't go to the trouble of preparing the cabbage and mash just for breakfast, but if you happen to have some left over from dinner or lunch this is a brilliant way of using it. Perhaps the next time you're having cabbage and mashed potato as part of a dinner or supper meal, cook a little extra for the morning.

Put the omelette pan over a medium heat and when hot add the goats' butter. When the goats' butter has melted add the egg and then carefully place the cabbage and potato mash in a line across the middle of the omelette. When the egg is still quite runny, but the omelette is sufficiently formed for you to lift an edge, fold one edge over the middle and the other across it. Carry on cooking for another minute, to make sure the bubble and squeak is warmed through, and serve.

Cheesy egg – in the microwave

eggs 2, beaten well

goats' or plant-based milk, whole, 1 glug

goats' butter, 1 knob

goats' or sheeps,' cheese grated, 1 good handful

Worcestershire sauce, 1 glug

1 portion, simply double up the quantities for 2

Beat the eggs in a microwavable Pyrex dish or similar and then add goats' or plant-based milk and stir, before adding goats' butter, goats' or sheeps' cheese and Worcestershire sauce.

Give a final stir, and put in the microwave for 30 seconds on high. Remove and stir, then put back for another 30 seconds and stir again.

You're looking to get this to the consistency of cottage cheese, so put back this time for 20 seconds and stir again, then another 20 seconds and stir again. Depending on the actual quantities that went in you're probably nearly there by now. So, cook for progressively shorter times until it is ready, stirring each time, and don't let it get too dry.

This is one of the easiest and tastiest ways of cooking eggs, especially for goats' or sheeps' cheese lovers.

Crabmeat omelette with spring onion and watercress

crabmeat, white, 2 handfuls, 100g – 150g (4oz – 6oz)

spring onion, 1, topped and tailed, thin sliced

watercress, chopped (stalks and all if you like a bit of crunch) 2 tablespoons

sheeps' or goats' yoghurt, 1 tablespoon

goats' butter, 1 knob

groundnut oil, 1 good glug

eggs, 4, well beaten

2 portions

Heat the frying pan over a medium heat and when quite warm add the oil and the goats' butter. When the goats' butter has melted and is sizzling spread it around the pan, add the crabmeat, spring onion and watercress and fry for 4 – 5 minutes when the crabmeat is beginning to brown. Remove the mixture from the pan with a slotted spoon and set aside in a bowl. Then add the sheeps' or goats' yoghurt to the crab mix and gently fold in.

Put the beaten eggs into the pan, and let the mixture begin to cook. After 1 minute add the crab mixture in a line across the centre of the omelette and cook for 2 minutes. Lift an edge with an egg slice and fold it over the middle, then lift the other edge and fold it across it. Carry on cooking for another minute, then turn allowing some of the egg to ooze out, and cook for a further 30 seconds.

Simply cut the omelette gently into 2, carefully remove from the pan and arrange on plates and serve.

NOTE: Cook the omelette for as long as you like, to suit your taste. Some people like the egg still runny, others like it well cooked. No hard and fast rules, just cook to your own taste. The timings above are in the middle.

Haddock chilli scramble

haddock fillet, 1, around 300g (¾lb)

eggs, 3

sheeps' or goats' yoghurt, 2 tablespoons

goats' butter, 3 knobs

shallot, 1, peeled and chopped

red chilli, tip only, with seeds if you like it very hot, chopped

groundnut oil, 1 glug

potato, medium, 1, skin on, diced into 4mm (1/8") pieces

purslane, chopped, 1 handful; try fennel stalk tops, tarragon, or chervil if you can't get it

salt, 2 good pinches

2 portions

Sounds a bit faffy but it isn't really, and it's a lovely breakfast, lunch or light supper. Some of the ingredients need cooking before the final cook as part of the preparation; it doesn't matter which ingredient you do first – if you can cope, cook them all at once.

Chillies make great house plants

The haddock needs pan-frying in 1 knob of goats' butter, so heat the pan over a medium heat then drop in the goats' butter. When melted place the haddock in the pan skin side down and fry for around 4 minutes before turning and then fry for another 4 minutes, then set aside and allow to cool. When cool, gently flake the fish off the skin into a mixture of different sized flakes.

Fry the shallot and chilli together in the groundnut oil until the shallot is soft and translucent, then scoop out onto kitchen towel to drain and set aside to cool.

Easily grown on a windowsill.

Heat frying pan over medium heat; when hot add 1 knob of goats' butter. When sizzling has stopped, add the potatoes and fry, stirring occasionally, for 5-10 minutes, until potatoes are golden brown. Scoop out to drain on kitchen towel.

Break the eggs into a bowl and beat them well, then add the salt, sheeps' or goats' yoghurt and last knob of goats' butter, then pour into a saucepan.

Now you're going to scramble the eggs, slowly, by using a wooden spoon to stir every few seconds and scraping the thickening egg mixture off the base and sides of the pan.

When the mixture is the consistency of double cream pour in the shallot chilli mix, and the potato. Continue stirring and scraping.

When the mixture is slightly more than the consistency of double cream gently place in the haddock flakes and continue stirring – carefully, to avoid breaking up the flakes too much - until the mixture is thick and the eggs are just about scrambled. Cook to taste really; some think creamier eggs are better than drier and some vice versa. As scrambled eggs thicken as they cool on the plate, I serve them creamy.

Now you're nearly finished – just pour the mixture onto 2 plates, sprinkle the purslane over and serve.

Scrambled egg and fish surprise breakfast

cod or haddock, ¼ - ½ fillet, pan-fried, cold, flaked off skin

new potatoes, medium, 2, boiled or steamed, diced

tip of chilli, seeds in, chopped

shallot, 1, peeled and chopped

purslane, handful, chopped, use parsley or a little chervil if you can't get purslane

goats' butter, 2 big knobs

spinach, 1 handful

salt, 2 good pinches

eggs, 4

whole goats' or plant-based milk or goats' or plant-based cream, 4 glugs

portions, 2

Surprise? – yes because we're using fish and potatoes left over from the previous night.

Start by making the scrambled egg mixture; beat the eggs in a Pyrex bowl and add 1 good pinch of salt, 1 big knob of goats' butter, and goats' or plant-based milk or goats' or plant-based cream.

Put on one side until the fish part is nearly finished.

Heat wok or large pan over medium heat and when hot add the goats' butter. When melted add the potato, chilli, shallot, 1 pinch of salt, and stir-fry. Stir-fry until the potato is beginning to turn golden brown and the chilli and shallot are cooked through. Stir-fry to avoid the chilli and shallot burning. When the potatoes are almost ready add the flaked fish, stir in, turn down the heat to low and begin cooking the scrambled egg in the microwave, as follows:

Cook on high for 40 seconds then remove, beat lightly to break up the thickening egg and return to the microwave. Then cook for another 40 seconds and remove and stir again, then in increments of 20 seconds, stirring after each – usually it will take 3 more removals and beatings to reach the nearly point, after which switch to 10 second stints. Watch for the end point carefully, especially if you like your scrambled egg moist, and remember it will carry on cooking even when it is out of the microwave because of its internal heat.

Just before removing the fish surprise from the pan add the spinach and stir in gently to avoid breaking up the fish, then pour the mixture onto plates closely followed by the scrambled egg.

Sprinkle the purslane over and enjoy a delicious and different way to use leftover fish; maybe a good reason for not eating all of it the night before!

Scrambled egg in the microwave

eggs, 4

goats' or plant-based milk, whole, 4 tablespoons

goats' butter, 2 good knobs

salt, 2 pinches

2 portions

Traditionalists out there will read on in horror, but this works really well, takes around 2 minutes, and avoids the risk of burning the egg on the bottom of the saucepan.

Just beat the eggs in a microwave safe bowl and add the salt, goats' butter, and your choice of non-dairy addition. This actually works really well with goats' or plant-based milk, but if you want a richer, smoother egg use goats' or plant-based cream or sheep or goats' or plant-based yoghurt. Put the bowl into the microwave on high for 40 seconds then remove, beat lightly to break up the thickening egg and return to the microwave for another 40 seconds, remove and beat lightly again.

Then return to the microwave and work in times of 20 seconds – usually it will take 3 more removals and beatings to reach the nearly point – when you're not sure if 20 seconds will be too long.

At that point reduce the time to 10 seconds. I like my scrambled egg quite runny so I watch the end point carefully.

If you think 10 seconds will be too long on the last run, simply open the microwave door and remove after 5 seconds to see. If necessary put back and give it another 5 or 10 seconds.

Serve immediately because if you leave it in the bowl for long it will carry on cooking and not end up on the plate with the consistency you've aimed for.

Tip – put water into the empty cooking bowl immediately, to stop the egg sticking to it.

Scrambled eggs work well with all sorts at breakfast, including smoked salmon or roasted tomatoes.

Scrambled egg, with roasted tomatoes

eggs, 4

goats' or plant-based milk or goats' or plant-based cream, 4 tablespoons

goats' butter, 2 good knobs

salt, 2 good pinches

tomatoes, 2, large

good olive oil, 2 glugs

2 portions

First, while the oven is heating to 180°C fan / gas mark 6, put the tomatoes on a baking tray and pour the oil over, rubbing to completely cover the skins. Put the tray in the oven for 25 minutes and just before removing them start scrambling the eggs.

The skins on the tomatoes will probably be split, and even if not, they'll be crispy and easy to remove, so do so now. Now slice them, using a board with a runnel round the edge, so you don't lose any of the juice, and cube them, removing the woody bits.

When the egg is cooked simply add the tomatoes and stir, then serve.

Smoked salmon and spring onion scramble with splotties

eggs, 4

smoked salmon, 2 slices, cut into bite sized pieces

spring onions, 4, topped and tailed, sliced

sheep or goats' yoghurt, 1 - 2 tablespoons

splotty mix, follow the recipe on page 89 for the method in *Sauces and Sides*

goats' butter, 1 good knob

2 portions

Lovely on a Sunday morning for brunch with a chilled glass of white wine, or even Champagne!

First make the splotties, and put in the oven on a low light to keep warm.

Add the goats' butter to a warmed pan and while still bubbling add the eggs and stir constantly, add the sheep or goats' yoghurt continuing to stir well. After around 3 minutes the egg will be almost cooked – you don't want it too dry – add the spring onions and smoked salmon, stir for another 30 seconds and you're ready to serve.

Smoky crab scramble

white and brown crabmeat, mixed, 100g, 4oz

natural smoked haddock, 1 small fillet, skin removed, cut into bite sized pieces

garlic, 2 cloves, crushed

spring onions, 3, chopped

new potatoes, 5, skin on and brushed to clean, small diced, into 6mm (¼") cubes

cherry tomatoes, 5, quartered

good olive oil, 1 good glug

coriander, fresh, with stalks, chopped, 1 handful

black pepper, freshly ground, lots, to taste

eggs, 3

salt, 1 large pinch

lemon, ½, juice of

2 large portions

Heat olive oil in a wok over medium heat and when hot add the potatoes and stir fry for about 10 minutes, until they are golden brown, then add the spring onions, salt, and garlic and fry for 5 more minutes, still stirring frequently.

Add tomatoes and smoked haddock and cook for 2 more minutes, still stirring frequently, and then add the coriander and lots of freshly ground black pepper; after 2 more minutes – yes, still stirring – add the crabmeat.

Now to scramble it; break the eggs, quickly one after the other, into the mixture, and stir constantly and vigorously for around 2 more minutes.

Tip onto two plates and gently squeeze a lemon over to taste................ Sublime...........what a way to start the day!

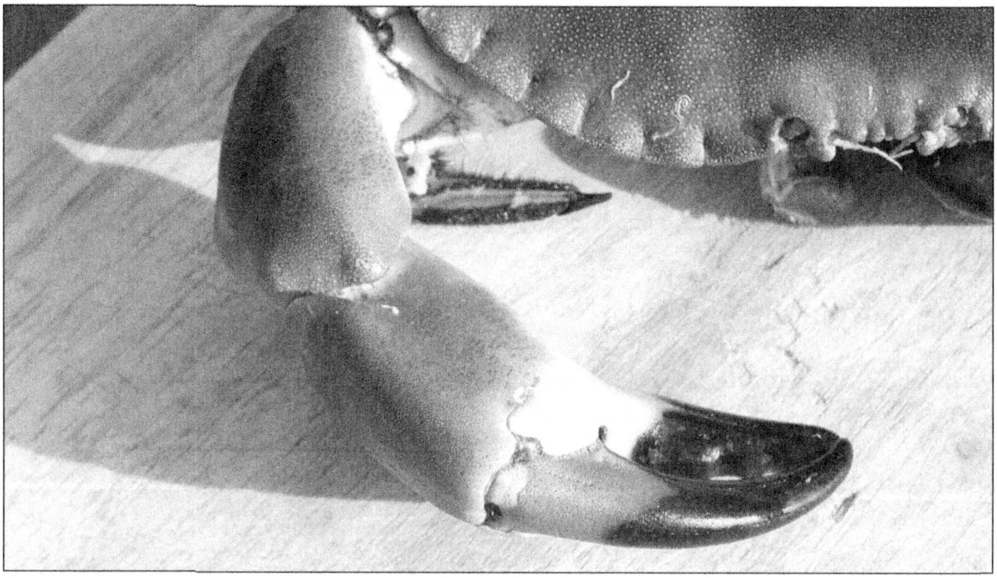

Fresh crab is great, a bit time consuming to pick, but then you've got the shell for an amazing stock!

Sorrel omelette

This is Mamá's favourite omelette and her comfort food

sorrel leaves, 9, 8cm long (3") or fewer larger leaves, stalk removed, torn into small pieces

eggs, 2, beaten with salt added

goats' butter, 1 good knob

salt, pinch to taste

1 portion

This really is so easy to make (if you have the sorrel of course, which can be grown really easily, with seeds being readily available from garden centres - it grows from February through to November in the greenhouse), and makes a change for breakfast. Sorrel is zingy, and adds a great citrusy flavour to the omelette.

First place an omelette pan on a medium heat, and when hot add the goats' butter. While the goats' butter is melting crack the eggs into a bowl and whisk well to make your omelette light, and the airing effect of whisking will make it very light. Add the salt, whisk for a few more seconds then add the egg to the pan.

Sprinkle the sorrel pieces onto the egg, mostly in a line across the middle, but dropping a few away from the centre. When the top of the omelette is still slightly runny, probably after around 30 seconds, lift one edge and fold it two thirds of the way across and then fold the other side over and serve straight away.

Omelettes are best cooked to be slightly runny when plated up; but you should cook to your own taste – if you like them well cooked just leave in the pan for longer and turn before sliding gently out onto the plate.

A refreshing light dish, taking just 2 – 3 minutes total to cook. As an alternative, add chopped skinned deseeded tomato flesh as well.

Tomato omelette

eggs, 2, beaten, with 1 pinch of salt

tomatoes, medium, 2, seeds removed, chopped, woody bits removed

goats' butter, 1 knob

2 portions

It is well worth removing the seeds from the tomatoes lest the resulting omelette be too runny. **BUT** try it with roasted tomatoes instead. Just roast whole tomatoes, drizzled with good olive oil, on medium heat for 25 minutes, take from oven and chop.

Put your omelette pan over a medium heat and when hot drop the goats' butter in. When the goats' butter has melted roll it around the pan before pouring the eggs in, then immediately sprinkle the tomato as evenly as you can over the egg.

After about 1½ - 2 minutes, when the omelette will be almost ready, fold one side over to the middle, then fold the other side over the first................and serve.

GLUTEN FREE BAKING

Cookies, oat crunch

Try these crumbled into plain goats', sheeps' or cows' yoghurt with a drizzle of honey

gluten free oats, 165gm, 6oz

caster sugar, 50gm, 1¾oz

dark soft brown sugar, 50gm, 1¾oz

demerara sugar, 30 gm, 1.25oz

vegetable oil, 125ml,

plain gluten free flour, 60 gm, just over 2 oz

egg, 1

baking powder, ½ teaspoon

table salt, ¼ teaspoon

portions. This will make around 12 cookies approximately 75mm, 3" in diameter

Feel free to experiment with different flavourings if you like, although I like this basic cookie. 1 teaspoon of vanilla essence can be added for example, or freshly ground black pepper, a teaspoon of dried ginger or cinnamon.

Pre heat the oven to 170°C fan / gas mark 5.

Simply mix all the dry ingredients in a large bowl and beat the egg with the oil in a jug. Pour from the jug into the bowl to combine the dry and wet ingredients and mix thoroughly. Place desertspoonfuls of the mixture onto a baking sheet lined with baking parchment leaving space between – about 5cm / 2" – to allow for spreading

Place the baking sheet in the oven for 15 minutes. Remove the sheet, the cookies will be a lovely golden brown. Allow to cool for 3 minutes before carefully lifting them from the sheet using a slice, as the cookies are fragile when hot, and place them on a cooling tray. If they have "merged", just separate with a knife whilst still on the baking sheet.

Crackers, with green or black olive chips

These are perfect with the Italian seafood pastes

gram flour, 40gm, just under 1½oz

gluten free self-raising flour, 190gm, 6¾ oz

olives, black or green, 17, stoned and fine chopped, or halved and processor whizzed

table salt, 1 teaspoon

caster sugar, 1 teaspoon

xanthan gum, 1/4 teaspoon

baking powder, 1 teaspoon

black pepper, 39 grinds of the mill

water, ½ cup, 125ml, 0.22 pint

extra virgin olive oil, 2 tablespoons

portions, this will make around 16 crackers approximately 30mm x 270mm long (1" x 9")

Mix dry ingredients in a bowl with a balloon whisk. Add the olives in a few batches mixing to incorporate into the flour. Add the oil and water and mix using a rubber spatula to form a dough.

Rest the dough for ½ hour. In the bowl on the side in the kitchen is fine.

Preheat oven to 200°C fan gas mark 7.

Place a sheet of baking parchment the right size for your baking tray on the kitchen counter, sprinkle liberally with gluten flour, roll into a rough rectangle around 2mm thick. Use plenty of flour to keep dusting the rolling pin, as gluten free flour is notorious for sticking!

Cut the rectangle into crackers the size and shape you are looking for, and LEAVE THEM ON THE PARCHMENT.

Gently lift the parchment onto a baking tray and place in the oven for around 15 minutes. Keep an eye on them. They may need a little longer until they have turned a soft, light brown.

Remove from the oven and gently lift the crackers onto a cooling tray.

NOTE – depending on the size of your baking tray you may need to do the baking in two batches, or to use 2 trays if you have them.

ANOTHER NOTE: - if the crackers are slightly softer than you like them after cooking, or they should turn softer, go for a second baking, at the same temperature for just 4 minutes to crisp them up. Don't worry, baking still seems to be a bit of an art form with the results being dependent on room temperature, humidity, and even the time of day of the baking!

Flaky pastry

goats' butter, from freezer, 150gm, 5.3oz

gluten free plain flour, 200gm, 7oz

xanthan gum, 2 large pinches

table salt, ½ teaspoon

water, cold, 10 – 12 tablespoons

portions. This makes sufficient pastry for two fish pasties (my recipe for this great pasty is on page 28), or around 16 mushy pea and cheese bites (my recipe for these delicious mini-pasties is on page 35).

Whisk the dry ingredients in a bowl. Coarse grate the butter, straight from frozen, sprinkling the grater with flour from time to time to maintain the edge. Mix using a cold metal palette knife until the mixture has the appearance of rough bread crumbs.

Add 8 tablespoons of water and mix using the palette knife, then continue adding and mixing water one tablespoon at a time until the dough can be formed. It should not be too dry, nor should it runny.

Roll the dough into a ball and wrap in cling film, leave in fridge for 30 minutes before rolling. I always give it five minutes to warm slightly before rolling. For pasties roll out directly on the baking parchment (having split your dough into two portions) you will be using to bake the pasties and use lots of gluten free plain flour on the parchment and the rolling pin to avoid sticking.

Use baking parchment with lots of gluten free plain flour on the parchment and rolling pin for the bites too, and a saucer to cut round to get the small circles of dough you need for the bites.

Cooking time is around 45 minutes for the pasties at 190°C fan / gas mark 6½ and 35 minutes for the bites.

Flatbread

Ideal with the fish curries and Eastern seafood stews

gram flour, ½ cup (100 gm, 4oz)

salt, a good pinch

water, 2/3 cup, (160ml, just under 0.3 pints)

olive oil, 2 tablespoons

portions, 2 flatbreads - fry separately using small frying pan

Sift the flour into a bowl, add salt, then whisk in 1/3 of the water until you have a thick paste with no lumps. Slowly whisk in the remaining water.

Heat a pan over a medium to hot heat, when hot add the oil. Pour in half the batter, cook for 2 – 3 minutes before using the largest slice you have to carefully flip the partially cooked bread and cooking the other side for 2 – 3 minutes. Repeat for the second bread.

The reason for splitting into two breads is to avoid a thicker bread, which may not be cooked all the way through. If you'd like it thicker and softer in the middle though try using all the batter in a medium sized pan

This goes really well with curry.

Pizza base, thin and crispy

gluten free bread flour, 190 gm, 7 oz

baking powder, 1 ½ teaspoons

table salt ½ teaspoons

caster sugar, 1½ teaspoons

xanthan gum, ¾ teaspoon

olive oil, 1½ teaspoons

water, 150ml, ¼ pint

portions This makes one 310mm, 12" diameter thin crust pizza base

Mix the ingredients well, leave to rest for ½ hour, just in a bowl in the kitchen is fine. Preheat oven to 240^{0} C fan, gas mark 8. You need a very hot oven.

Remove dough from bowl onto baking parchment on a board and hand press into circular shape to fit your pizza baking tray. Place the pizza tray, inverted over the dough and flip the base onto the pizza tray. Peel off the Baking parchment. Bake in the hot oven for 5 minutes.

Allow to cool before adding toppings. Once you have loaded the base with the toppings of your choice, place back in the reheated oven for around 15 minutes.

One of my very favourite toppings is a bit off the wall – a mushy pea base (my mushy pea recipe is on page 80) instead of tomato paste, with prawn and fish on top along with red onions, green pepper green olives and capers!

Soda Bread

This loaf can be used for breadcrumbs wherever they are called for. Just cut a thick slice and finely chop. If you don't need them all, just freeze.

gluten free bread flour, 550 gm

baking powder, 3½ teaspoons

xanthan gum, 1 teaspoon

lemon juice, 1½ tablespoons

bicarbonate of soda, 1½ teaspoons

salt, 1½ teaspoons

clear runny honey, 2 teaspoons

sheeps' (or goats') yoghurt, 550 ml

Portion, makes 1 loaf

Unlike most soda breads which are round, I prefer to make mine looking more like a conventional loaf, so I use a traditional 1kg/2lb loaf tin for the baking. Of course you can use the tin that suits you best.

Pre heat the oven to 190°C fan / gas mark 6½.

Heat the yoghurt in a saucepan or the microwave until it is warm to the touch – 60 seconds full power in my microwave. Add the lemon juice and honey and stir well.

Whisk all the dry ingredients together in a mixing bowl, add the yoghurt mix and stir to amalgamate. Sometimes I need to add a little goat's milk or plant-based milk to take up all the flour mix.

No resting!

Tip and spoon the dough into the baking parchment lined tin – easiest with custom-made loaf tin liners - and smooth the top then stab the loaf with a knife or skewer all over right to the bottom. This lets the air out during cooking and helps to avoid splitting. I find scalding the knife or skewer with boiling water helps it slide out without dragging the dough with it.

When the oven is up to temperature put in your tin and leave for 31 minutes.

Take the bread from the oven, remove it from the tin and put it onto a cooling tray.

There may well be a split in the loaf, don't worry, this is normal!

And finally

Critters

I have chosen to close this little book with my all-time favourite recipe. I still make this at least once a week - more often twice or three times - when courgettes and garden mint are in season. Born in the summer, I have them every birthday for breakfast with poached eggs.

Oh by the way, there are no creatures involved here; when I was little I struggled to pronounce the letter 'F', so courgette fritters became 'critters' and the name stuck, being used by my family ever since.

courgettes, 2, medium, skins on, grated using a coarse grater onto 2 tea towels, one on top of the other.

common or garden mint leaves, centre veins cut out, good handful finely chopped

plain gluten free flour, 2 tablespoons

salt, 1½ teaspoons to 'dust' the grated courgettes

ground white pepper, plenty, to taste

eggs 1, beaten

vegetable oil, 1 glug

Goats' butter, 1 good knob

tea towels, 2

2 portions

The grated courgettes contain a lot of moisture, most of which needs removing which is why you've grated them onto tea towels. First sprinkle the salt over the courgettes and toss them to mix in the salt as evenly as possible. Spread the grated courgette evenly over the tea towels. and leave to stand for 30 minutes. The tea towels will then be quite soggy and the courgettes can be squeezed to expel excess moisture. You need them as dry as possible.

Move the grated courgettes to the centre of the tea towels, gather the corners together in one hand like a Christmas pudding parcel, take to the sink or a bowl and ring them out by holding the courgette end and twisting it. Moisture will drip from the tea towels. When the moisture has been pretty much drained (you are looking for pretty dried out courgettes at this stage), open the tea towels and carefully tip the courgettes into a bowl, scraping the final gratings from the tea towel.

Add the flour, mint and pepper and mix well. At this point, BEFORE adding the egg, the critter mixture can be frozen. This is better than freezing the finished, precooked, critters. When you're ready to use the frozen mix, defrost naturally before adding the egg and carry on as below.

Add the egg and mix well. Now form the mixture by hand into the sizes and shapes of critter you want to appear when cooked, around 15mm (a bit less than ¾") thick. I like them around 100mm (4") in diameter. Then put them on a plate and leave in the fridge to chill for 30 minutes. A bit more won't harm them.

Heat a frying pan over medium heat and when hot add the vegetable oil then the butter. When melted swirl butter round to cover base of pan and gently, using a slice or similar, place the critters in the pan. Cook for around 5 – 7 minutes then gently turn them. The cooked side should be a lovely golden brown. Cook the other side for 5 -7 minutes.

Now simply place them onto a baking sheet and into a warm oven (Fan 160°C ,gas mark 4) for 15 minutes or so until the remainder of your meal is ready to serve. This will ensure the centres are cooked through properly as well as keeping them warm.

I hope you enjoy the Critters as much as I still do after all these years!!

I do hope you enjoyed my Little Cornish Cookbook . Read on for more about me, my brother DI Félipe Treloar (I call him Flip), and his challenges as told in the Cornish crime thriller series written by L. A. Kent.

Beatriz Treloar

An Egret, caught stalking in Mevagissey harbour

More about Beatriz Treloar and the DI Treloar Cornish Crime Thrillers

About Beatriz Treloar

Beatriz Treloar is the exciting young head chef at SEAFOOD ON STILTS and THE CUTTLEFISH CAFE in St Ives, Cornwall. She first appears in the second DI Treloar crime thriller, the award-winning BROKEN DOVE.

Situated on the quayside in St Ives, the restaurant sits above the café's terrace – hence the stilts. Beatriz is the youngest of DI Félipe Treloar's three sisters.

About the DI Treloar Cornish Crime Thrillers

The DI Treloar series written by L A Kent follows the exploits of the detective as he and his team face serious, challenging crimes in Cornwall. There are four books to date with a fifth, FALLEN KESTREL, the Marazion Murders, to be published in late 2022 or early 2023:

Rogue Flamingo – The Mevagissey murders

Broken Dove – The St Ives murders

Silent Gull – The Fowey murders

Sad Pelican – The Padstow murders

To get your Cornish murder mystery reading juices flowing the book covers are on the next page. They are available as paperbacks and can be bought from bookshops and Amazon, as well as Kindle editions.

The Cornish setting book covers are shown overleaf and you can read more about LA Kent and the strong-minded and some would say maverick DI Treloar at www.lakent.co.uk.

Here are the DI Treloar series book covers to whet your appetite, just go to Amazon or your favourite bookshop to get your copies!

Copyright

ISBN 9798373387347

Published by WillowOrchard Publishing

The authors also publish under the pseudonym L. A. Kent, writing crime thrillers – the DI Treloar Cornish crime thriller series. Beatriz Treloar is DI Treloar's sister. You can read more about the series and subscribe to the L. A. Kent news updates on the web site www.lakent.co.uk. You will receive a free dossier written by HM Secret Services on DI Treloar when you subscribe to the newsletter.

Index

Printed in Great Britain
by Amazon

26598585R00077